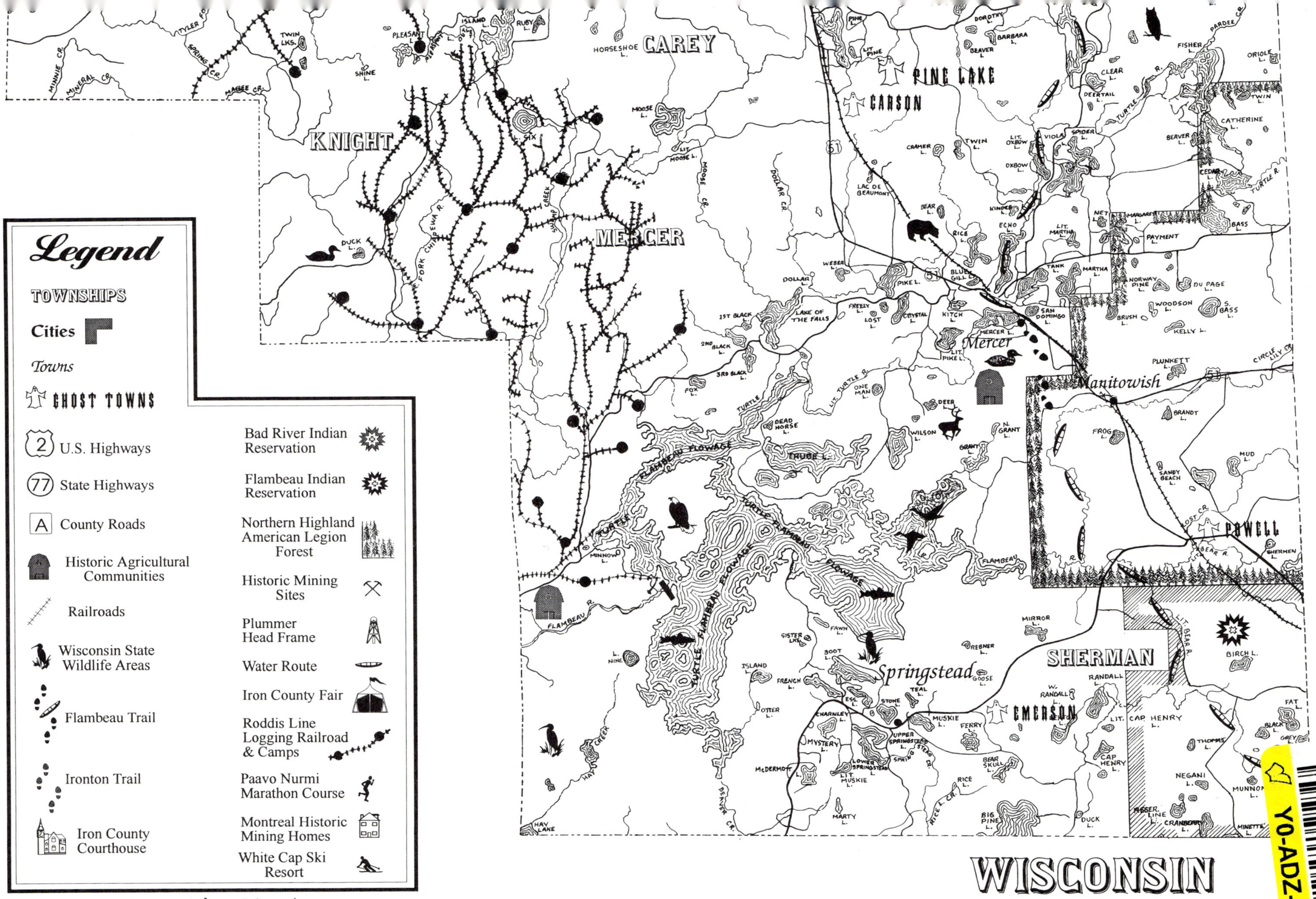

1993 Image Advertising Agency

ROOTED IN RESOURCES

Rooted in Resources
Iron County, Wisconsin 1893-1993

Catherine Techtmann

Copyright 1993, Iron County, Wisconsin and New Past Press, Inc.

All Rights Reserved

All rights reserved. No part of this book may be reproduced in any form or by any electronic or mechanical means including information storage and retrieval systems without permission in writing from the publisher, except by a reviewer who may quote brief passages in a review.

Funding
Iron County, Wisconsin

Publishing Services
Research, Writing, Editing, Design, Art, Pre-Press Production

New Past Press Inc., Friendship, Wisconsin

Editing: Michael J. Goc
Publishing Assistant, Page Design: Carol Ann Podoll, Friendship, Wisconsin
Cover Design: Kristie Cecil, Stevens Point, Wisconsin
Maps: Larry D. Peterson Studios, Ironwood, Michigan

Printing
Weber & Sons, Inc., Park Falls, Wisconsin

Manufactured in the United States of America

ISBN 0-938627-18-X

Library of Congress Cataloging in Publication

Techtmann, Catherine, 1951-
    Rooted in resources: Iron County, Wisconsin, 1893-1993/ by Catherine Techtmann.
    p. 160
    1. Iron County (Wis.) --History. 2. Iron County (Wis .) -Industries. I. Title
F587.17T43   1993
977.5'22-dc20   93-3553   CIP

Dedication

"Rooted in Resources" is dedicated to the people who shaped Iron county's past and to those with the vision to forward its future.

Table of Contents

Introduction	6
Acknowledgments	7
Rooted in Resources	8
The People of the County	42
Making a Living on Main Street	48
Moving People and Words	70
City and County Schools	76
Faiths Diverse	82
Good Times	86
Extra! Extra!	102
Government in the County	112

Table of Contents

County Municipalities 116

Anderson	118
Carey	120
Gurney	122
Hurley	126
Kimball	128
Knight	130
Mercer	132
Montreal	134
Oma	136
Pence	138
Saxon	140
Sherman	142

Iron County Chronicle 144
Index 158
Afterword 160

Introduction

This book takes a different look at Iron county's history. We have chosen to interpret the major historic themes of the county as a whole area, stressing the common history we share. Rather than recapitulate historic facts, we have tried to capture the zest of the people who shaped Iron county. Photos and captions tell the story.

Iron county's history is too rich to be completely covered in one volume. It is our hope that this book sparks an appreciation of our history and the role it can play in the development of Iron county.

Rich natural resources, like iron and timber, provided fertile ground for Iron county's early development to take root. But the future does not only lay in the colorful past or remembrances of boom days of yesteryear. It is rooted in the history that we make today.

Of all of its natural resource treasures, Iron county's greatest resource will prove to be its people.

Iron County Centennial Book Committee

Acknowledgments

The preparation of this book was like the discovery of iron ore; it came as a "boom". The catalyst was County Board Chairman Louis Leoni who believed it was important to document the county's first 100 years in a special centennial book. The Iron County Economic Development Committee was given charge of the project.

Local historians, representing all areas of the county, volunteered to serve on the Centennial Book Committee. Manuscript preparation and coordination of "Rooted in Resources" was done by the Iron County University of Wisconsin-Extension Office. The Centennial Committee had less than four months to compile research, find historic photos, and write the manuscript for the book to be ready for distribution by June 1993.

Realizing the magnitude of the project, a call for help went out to the public. The response was nothing short of amazing. People opened their homes, family histories, and memoirs. Local historical societies in Iron county and neighboring counties made their precious research and photo collections available. Many of the photos and facts in this book came from these sources and have not been seen in any other publication.

Letters and phone calls of support encouraged us as we took on the big task of compiling 100 years of Iron County's history. Neighbors volunteered to find last-minute pieces of information. Volunteers burned the midnight oil to write and proofread the manuscript in order to get it to the publisher by the deadline.

Special recognition must be given to the late Otto Erspamer and Armand Cirilli. From their extensive collections of newspaper clippings, photographs, and memoirs, much of this book was written. Thanks to their foresight and dedication to preserve Iron County's history, its legacy will continue.

The project was funded by a grant from Iron County and by contributions of $250 each from the following municipalities: Towns of Sherman, Anderson, Kimball, Knight, Oma, Saxon, Gurney, Mercer and Pence; Cities of Montreal and Hurley.

Every attempt has been made to accurately report the dates and events of Iron county's history. Sometimes, however, accuracy fades with time. We apologize for any discrepancies between what is presented here and what might appear in other histories or personal remembrances.

We express our sincere thank you to the many people who contributed remembrances, family photos, and the moral support that made this book possible. Among those who were instrumental in making "Rooted in Resources" a reality:

Special Thanks to the Iron County Centennial Book Committee
Nelle Kopacz, Historical research; Mitch Babic, Mercer area history, proofreading; Norman and Joan Pripps, Springstead area history; Larry Peterson, Historical research, map work, proofreading; Craig Lewis, Historical research, proofreading; Clyde Eilo, Historical research; Cathy Techtmann, Manuscript preparation, coordination.

And
Linda Ryskewecz, Proofreading, manuscript preparation; Michael Goc, Editor and publisher; Iron County Historical Society, Nelle Kopacz; Mercer Historical Society, Shirley Sleight; Ironwood Carnegie Library, Joanne Fleming; Iron County Miner, Ernie Moore, Bill Moore; Ironwood Daily Globe; Mercer Department of Natural Resources Station, Dave Sleight; Gilbert Endrizzi Photo Collection; Otto Erspamer Collection; Armand Cirilli Collection; Cory Winn, for Centennial logo design; Earle E. Sell; Iron County Economic Development Committee; Iron County Board of Supervisors; Lac du Flambeau Tribal Museum; Price County Historical Society, George Koshak, Pat Schroeder; City of Park Falls Public Library; Ashland Historical Society; State Historical Society of Wisconsin

Photo Credits
Gib Endrizzi, Mitch Babic, Craig Lewis, Larry Peterson, Otto Erspamer Collection, Paul Niemi, Dick Bugni, George and Charlotte Koshak, John Hakala, John Kostac, Kenneth Meyer, Carol Striegel, Jim Kaffine, Ray Maurin, Alphonse Zanella, Joe Innis, Barbara Innes, Tom Popko, Joan Giovanoni, Wilma Kauppi, John Sola, Sr., Charles Ahlgrim, Joyce Bednar, Joan and Norman Pripps, Carol Hanneman, Herb Nikula, Dr. Neal Schroeter, Pastor J. Pavel, Clyde Eilo, Carl Prosek, Sonya Luoma, Mercer Schools, Verner Thompson, William Mattson Family, Charles Raymond, Val Gene Coxey, Sue Abelson, Cy Sorrels, Dick Rowe, Audrey Clark, Albin Seifert, Mrs. Evert Seifert, H. Lee Olson, Mary Ann Brown, Iron County Miner and Ernie Moore, Ironwood Daily Globe and Gerard Lauzon, Iron County Historical Society, Ashland Historical Society, Price County Historical Society, State Historical Society of Wisconsin, St. Louis County, Minnesota, Historical Society, Mercer DNR Ranger Station, Lac du Flambeau Museum, Iron County Extension Office

A sincere Thank You to all of the families, businesses, and individuals who offered photos for this book. We regret that space limits the inclusion of all the photos that were submitted.

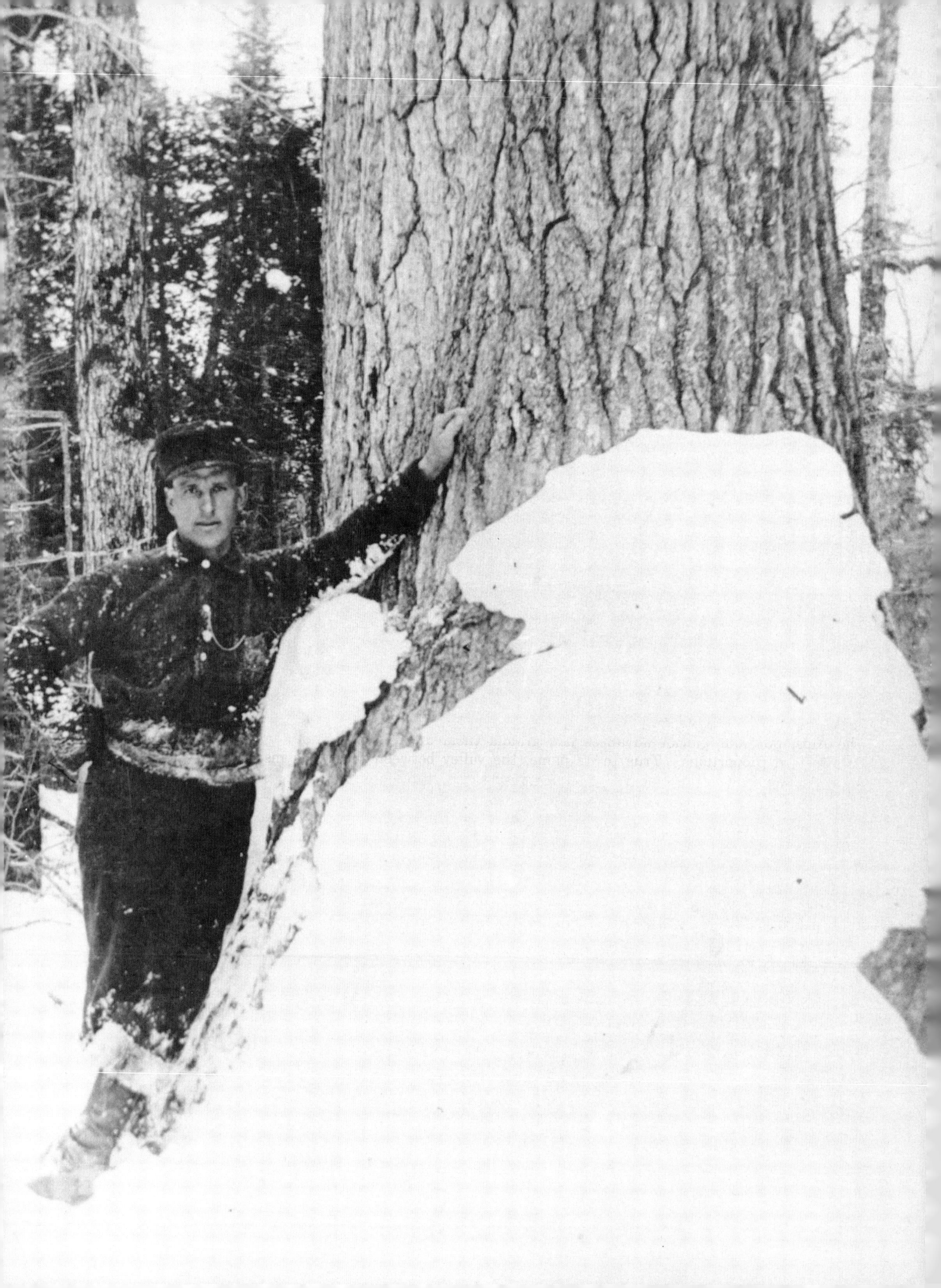

Rooted in Resources

Before the first footsteps of Native Americans, before the explorers, loggers, miners, and settlers, the destiny of the area we know as Iron county had been determined by the wealth of its natural resources. The legacy of Iron county is rooted in its resources and intertwined with the people who sought to link their future with its wealth.

Iron county is a land of contrasts. In the north, the country rises from the red clay basin of Lake Superior to a spine of rugged mountains. Charles Whittlesey, while conducting a geologic survey of Wisconsin in 1850, called them the "Penokee" Mountains, a misspelling of the Chippewa word "Pewabic" or iron. The Penokees were once as high as the Alps, but four glacial advances had ground them down to "mountains" of only Midwestern proportions. True to its name, the valley between the two arms of the Penokee Mountains would yield some of the world's richest iron ore.

The landscape of southern Iron county is more gentle and rolling. The pine, maple and aspen forest covering the sandy uplands is interspersed with nearly 200 lakes, bogs, and swamps. Free-flowing rivers like the Manitowish (also known as the East Branch of the Chippewa River), Turtle, and Flambeau are linked by lakes, making them ideal water trails. These rivers flow south, joining other waterways leading to the Chippewa and eventually the Mississippi River.

Water was the resource that dictated the early transportation and commerce of Iron county. It was much easier to float goods and people by bateau or canoe along river "highways" like the Manitowish, Turtle, and Flambeau than it was to fight the dense forests and rugged overland trails.

If the southern half of the county is rich in water resources, the rugged northern half is stingy. Inland lakes are few. The rivers that drain the country flow northward, dropping with a gradient as steep as 70 feet to the mile in their headlong rush through the Penokees down to Lake Superior. As they tumble over rock outcroppings, they create

---

Montreal, 1907. Pioneer logger Anton Bugni of Hurley stands beside a huge white pine found south of Montreal. Starting in the late 1870s, stands of virgin pine like this giant were cut, to provide the resources to establish sawmills such as the Mead, McLaughlin Company of Hurley. By 1907, the last sizable stands of pine were already logged, save for isolated trees like this one. Sawyers had to build a scaffold to cut it since a seven-foot saw would not reach through the tree at its base. The first log from this remnant giant measured 6'4" in diameter.

Upson, c. 1890. The Sackett family enjoys the Potato River for a family outing. (l-r, in the river) Jim Colenso, George Sackett (standing), and Emory Sackett, (seated on large rock) Emma Sackett, the Sackett baby, and another Sackett (holding fishing pole). Families often traveled to the waterfalls north of Hurley, Lake Lavina, Rock Cut in Kimball, and Lake of the Falls in Mercer to picnic, fish and be refreshed by Iron county's natural beauty.

beautiful but impassable waterfalls and rapids. So fierce was their flow that, over time, they eroded the resistant volcanic rock of the Penokee Range, carving notches called watergaps. These tumultuous waterways might have become a direct link to the Great Lakes and the world beyond, via the St. Lawrence Seaway, but they were not navigable.

Accentuating the differences between the two ends of the county, in the middle lies the Northern Highland Continental Divide. Surface waters to the north of this geologic "demarcation line" flow to Lake Superior; to the south, to the Mississippi River.

Travelers coming from the south knew they could find relatively easy and cheap water transportation in Iron county. In the north, however people and goods had to travel overland, using rough trails that followed the river valleys.

▶ Lake Superior Bluffs, Saxon. Shallow waters at the foot of steep red clay bluffs limited the size of vessels that could be safely docked and offered meager refuge from the north winds that buffeted Iron county's Lake Superior shore. Without a good natural harbor, Iron county could not become the site of a major Great Lakes port.

▼ Mouth of the Montreal, July 2, 1820. "We arrived at the mouth of the Montreal from where we could see a beautiful waterfall of about 70 feet ... A little above the river on the lake shore are several lodges of Indians on a piece of level ground bounded on three sides by mountains through which a creek flows"- James Doty, member of the Henry Schoolcraft territorial survey party.

▲ Cut from conglomerate rock, the rapids and falls of the 300-foot deep Montreal River Canyon were two of the many obstacles that made the Montreal River unsuitable as a waterway into Iron county. Small boats and canoes carried trade goods from Lake Superior to the mouth of the Montreal River, then portaged inland on the Flambeau Trail, around the edge of the canyon. They then came south, roughly following the course of the Gogogashugun River, or west branch of the Montreal.

11

Saxon, c. 1915. Paul Niemi, Saxon pioneer, logger, and trapper. Like other settlers, Niemi relied on wildlife for food, pelts and profit, if fur prices were good.

▼ Mercer, 1940. Until the late 1800s, beaver populations in the wilds of North America fluctuated according to the whims of fashion in Europe and the eastern United States. Felt made from Iron county beaver was fashioned into the plumed chapeaux favored by the kings of France and the stovepipe hats worn by American Presidents. When taste and materials changed, the demand for beaver declined. Populations recovered, but were hard-pressed again during the Depression of the 1930s. The beaver came back again and, in 1993, there are probably as many beaver in Iron county as when the first white trapper arrived.

In 1659, French explorers Pierre d'Esprit le Sieur Radisson and Medard Chouart le Sieur Groselliers arrived in the Chequamegon area to help build a successful fur trading empire for the French. Beaver pelts were the hot commodity. Processed into fashionable felt hats much in demand in Europe, beaver fur was the key commodity of the North American fur trade.

Far from being isolated, the Chippewa people living in Iron county were already part of a great continental trading network. They bartered locally-gathered commodities--copper from the Upper Peninsula, furs, foodstuffs--to other tribes to the south and east for 150 years before the first white American arrived.

Radisson and Groselliers may have been the first non-Indians to set foot in Iron county. They report that they followed their Chippewa guides south from Lake Superior [through Iron county] along the Flambeau Trail "to win ye shortest way to their nation at Lac du Flambeau".

Over the 45-mile Flambeau Trail, the equivalent of millions of dollars of beaver pelts were moved overland or by canoe during the fur trading era. In the late 1700s, goods moved up the Trail from the Northwest Company post at Lac du Flambeau to the mouth of the Montreal River and on to La Pointe, Quebec and Europe.

Francois Victor Malhoit, a 28-year-old clerk for the Northwest Fur Company, passed through Iron county on the Flambeau Trail in 1804, enroute to Lac du Flambeau to spend the winter trading with the Chippewa. With birch bark canoes loaded with flour, port, 20 kegs of rum and high wines, powder, shot, bullets, other trade goods, and seven voyageurs, he started his assignment from Fort Williams, Canada on the north shore of Lake Superior.

He paddled along the Lake's shoreline until he reached the mouth of the Montreal River. Here, the trade goods were loaded into backpacks for the overland trek to Long Lake. Each voyageur carried two packs weighing 80 to 90 pounds over the "120 pause" portage, so named for the number of times the voyageurs stopped to take a rest; about once every half-mile. Depending on the trail's condition, the load to be carried, and the motivation level of the travelers, the portage could take between 2.5 to 7 days.

So dense were the forests of Iron county and rugged the terrain that Malhoit exclaimed, "The portage trail is narrow, full of overturned trees, obstacles, muskeg, ... inhabited solely by owls because no other animal could find a living there."

The journey is an arduous one. Observing his men, "How weak they are! I gave each man a drink of shrub, two double handfuls of flour, and two pounds of pork which they began to eat with such avidity that I was twice obliged to take the dish away from them; fortunately, they all escaped with slight twinges of colic."

Caribou, elk, moose, wolverine, bear, and wolves were among the wildlife species that inhabited the old growth forests of Iron county. By the 1850's, with their habitat radically altered, many of these species would disappear. Different species--whitetail deer, coyote--that could survive in the Cutover and tolerate greater pressure from humans would take their place in a new ecosystem.

Saxon. ca. 1910. (l-r) Axel Niemi, a boy named "Beano", and an unidentified young man. Most of the pines cut during the heyday of logging were over 100 feet tall. What is typically considered "virgin timber" now is usually less than 100 years old, and dates to the earliest settlement period.

Across northern Wisconsin stretched an immense forest of pine and hardwoods. On the lighter, sandy soils of southern Iron county and in scattered belts in the north, forests of pine reaching over 100 feet tall towered over an understory of smaller hemlock, sugar maple, and shade-tolerant shrubs. Vast stands of maple, birch, and basswood grew on the heavier loam soils. On the edges of the marshes and bogs stood spruce, fir, and tamarack.

The Chippewa ceded their land to the United States between 1829 and 1854, opening the way for the development of northern Wisconsin by white Americans. By the 1860s, the "splendid forests" of northern Wisconsin were viewed as a new source to supply the growing demand for boards, shingles, and lath needed to build the rapidly growing cities and farms of the Midwest. White pine--lightweight, strong, free of knots--was the first choice of sawyers and builders.

The new state of Wisconsin was land rich, but revenue poor. Huge tracts of northern Wisconsin land were sold to the highest bidder to raise capital for the state. Shrewd capitalists, speculators, and downstate sawmill operators saw the investment potential and bought prime parcels of pine-covered public land within the new territory at auction for minimum bids of $1.25 per acre. The Wisconsin Central Railroad and the state university were awarded millions of acres of land to be resold to help fund construction and development. Plain folks looking for a forty or two usually got what was left--land without prime timber that they purchased by "private entry" sales after the auction. They could also purchase land from real estate companies, the railroads, or at a tax sale.

The felling of Iron county's white pine began in the late 1870s. Down the same south-flowing rivers that carried the voyageurs, buoyant white pine logs were floated to

Private "jobbers" were also contracted to cut logs for logging companies and operated camps around the county. The tools of the trade may be different, but today's loggers contend with the same rigors of hard, hazardous work, uncooperative weather, and difficulties in transporting logs to market as the pioneers.

Park Falls, c. 1880. A wannigan stuck in a chute of the Park Falls dam, during a log drive on the North Fork of the Flambeau. Pine logs from Iron county were floated to mills many miles downstream on the Flambeau and the Chippewa. Wannigans served as the cook shanty and bunk house for the drivers. Contrary to popular belief, the loggers did not "ride" the logs on the entire 200-mile trip downstream. Instead, they followed the drive in the sharp-prowed "bateaux" (at the left) and used them to return upstream.

sawmills in Ladysmith, Chippewa Falls, Eau Claire, and later, Park Falls.

North of the continental divide, logs could be floated or moved over the frozen rivers only as far as the Penokee Range would allow. Sawmills like the Mead, McLaughlin Company of Hurley in 1886, the VanBuskirk Brothers Sawmill in 1889 in Oma, and the Montreal River Lumber Company in Gile in 1890 established their operations along the branches of the Montreal River to take advantage of its water resources.

Winter was the season when logs could be most easily cut and moved over iced roads by horse teams to "landings" on the rivers. The lumber companies purchased large tracts of pine to supply their mills and operated large lumber camps employing as many as 500 men in the woods. The French-Canadians pine loggers who briefly settled in Sherman and claimed the 160 acres allotted by the Homestead Act of 1862, stayed only long enough to cut pine, whether it was on their allotment or not. They used oxen to haul logs to the stream banks and float them down the Flambeau.

Spring, when the rivers were at their highest, was the easiest time to float logs to a mill. To insure a consistent flow of water, a series of dams, such as Shea's Dam on the Turtle River north of Mercer, was constructed to provide the flush of water needed to carry the logs downstream. Logs were prodded into the fast-moving rivers by the drivers who would skip from log to log to steer the big sticks with their pike poles through the dams and down the chute on their journey to the mill.

The colorful pinery days were intense but short in Iron county. The first drive of logs on the North Fork of the Flambeau River took place in the late 1870s. By 1906, the last sizable stands of pine had been cut. Gus Hosley is credited with the last drive, of cedar logs, down the Flambeau River in 1904 or 1905.

Island Rapids, North Fork of the Flambeau River, 1920. From the fur trading days through the pinery era, rivers like the Manitowish, Turtle, and Flambeau served as the highways over which natural resources flowed from Iron county to markets in the south. The coming of the railroad and depletion of white pine ended the colorful river driving days, leaving the rivers to recreational paddlers. Traces of the old logging dams and pine "deadheads" that were left behind can still be found along these waterways.

Hoatz Camp, Sandhill, Oma c. 1900. Scores of logging camps sprang up during the heyday of logging prior to World War I and continued to be used until World War II. Early camps were built on the railroad main line, but as the timber was cut, they moved farther into the woods along short railroad spurs. Despite their rough-and-tumble image, many camps were operated by families who contracted both with loggers and the railroad to cut and transport logs. Logging was rigorous, manual labor–work for vigorous young men.

Most of the white pine was cut by the turn of the century, but vast stands of valuable hardwood remained throughout the county. Hardwood presented a different problem for the logger. It did not float like pine or cedar, so it had to be transported overland to mills. Most mills were too far from the supply of timber and the country was too rugged to make hauling feasible with horses or oxen. Accordingly the hardwood forest stood largely untouched until the arrival of the railroad.

The resource wealth of Iron county had not gone unnoticed. As early as the 1850s, settlers and speculators had called for the construction of a railroad through the central part of Wisconsin to Lake Superior. Bolstered by grants that offered up to ten sections or 6,400 acres for every mile of track laid, and exemptions from all property taxes for five years, railroads like the Milwaukee Lake Shore and Western and the Wisconsin Central extended their lines north to capitalize on the opportunities found in Iron county.

To harvest the virgin stands of hardwoods, hemlock, aspen, and remaining pine, lumber companies like Roddis, Hines, and the Dells built their own "logging railroads" out from a main track and deep into Iron county.

William Henry Roddis teamed up with the Wisconsin Central Railroad in 1903 to build a standard gauge rail line to export timber from Iron and Ashland counties to his Marshfield mill and, later, another mill in Park Falls. The Wisconsin Central Railroad profited from the deal through increased freight traffic and the sale of timber from its own extensive granted lands. New settlers who would, presumably, follow the rail line into the new country would also travel and ship goods on the new line.

By 1938, the Roddis Line boasted fifty miles of track, with spurs spreading like branches into northwestern Iron county as far north as Lake O'Brien and east to Island Lake and the confluence of the Turtle and Manitowish Rivers.

The Roddis line was dotted with logging camps. Roddis employed as many as 1,000 men at Park Falls, in its own logging camps and through logging contractors. Roddis Company camps, like "Camp 12," were numbered. Camps operated by contractors, such as the Nelson and Corrigan Camps, were named for the contractor.

Accommodations at the camps were spartan, but adequate: a bunk house or two, a cook shanty, office, blacksmith shop, filing shack, horse barn, pig pens, a small store called a "wannigan" named for the floating cookshack of the river drivers, and perhaps an engine house and coal bin. When the timber nearby was cut, the camp was closed and, to reduce fire hazards, all buildings destroyed or moved.

Staples Mill, c. 1900. As the pinery declined, the E & H Staples Mill used another locally-available wood resource, cedar, to manufacture shingles. The shingle mill offered light work and jobs for young boys hired to stencil the product's name–"E & H Staples Standard A"–on the bundles of shingles.

Mercer, 1896. Sometimes water and rail transportation were both used to transport logs. These logs were floated down the Turtle River from the Fisher Lake country to the south end of Echo Lake. Once there, a hoist lifted them out of the water and loaded them onto flat cars for shipment to nearby mills.

Springstead area, 1908. One of the Emerson brothers, in the fur coat, poses atop a sleigh of pine. Most logging and hauling was done in the winter. "Ice" roads were built from the timber to the rail spur. After a right-of-way had been cleared, a "rutter" pulled by horses or oxen cut two parallel tracks of the same gauge as the logging sleigh. Wagons loaded with water followed the rutters and dipped water into the ruts, creating a fixed, slick track for the logging sleighs.

Pine Lake Landing, c. 1930. The railroad meant that logging was no longer limited to the winter. Logs, like this hardwood timber, could be cut and moved by sleigh and stockpiled at rail spurs during the winter months for shipment to market by rail in the spring and summer. Stockpiled logs were piled high on "rollaways" alongside the tracks. When the train stopped, a steam-powered "jammer" was used to load logs.

    The company peaked during the 1920's economic boom, with fourteen camps full of lumberjacks cutting hemlock, maple, birch, and cedar. The Great Depression ended the boom. Camp 15, the last of the railroad camps, closed in 1938. After 35 years, the Roddis Line hauled its last load. World War II stimulated demand for plywood and made work for Roddis. The company became the largest supplier of plywood products to the military during the war; most certainly, some of the wood came from Iron county. By 1947, the vast supply of timber was exhausted and demand for plywood reduced. In 1956, Roddis sold the last of its Cutover land and ended its 53-year history of logging in Iron county.

    No more than a handful of settlers followed the Roddis line into the woods. No new towns or farms were created. Today all that can be found of the Roddis line are the traces of the old railroad grades and the brush clearings where the camps once stood.

    Timber helped to "open up" the country. By the late 1880s, railroads linked Iron county to more prosperous markets. Jobs in the woods brought new settlers. Communities sprang up around the mills and logging camps that just a few years earlier had been wilderness. Fortunes were made by those with the resources and the gumption to gamble on the wealth that could be made in lumber.

Saxon, c. 1900. A network of rail spurs linked the logging camps to mills and markets beyond the county's boundaries via mainline tracks of the Duluth, Atlantic and South Shore, the Milwaukee Lake Shore and Western, and the Wisconsin Central Railroads. Railroads made it possible to move logs to market all year round.

On the Roddis Line, c. 1903. "Old Kate" was the first engine used by the Roddis Company. Pictured are Joe Corrigan, Byron Mason, and Mert Hayward. The Roddis Line ran with only one locomotive for its first ten years of operation. Logging trains were usually limited to 10 cars pulled by only one locomotive. Practically all of the traffic transported on the Roddis Line consisted of logs, except in 1925 when earth fill was hauled to build the dike for the Turtle Flambeau Flowage.

The steam hauler, also known as a "slide ass," replaced horses in some logging operations. Whole trainloads of logs could be hauled to the rail spur, instead of just one sleighload at a time. The steam hauler was steered from the front and rode on wooden skis.

But a price was paid for the wealth the forests yielded. By the 1930s, the wellspring of timber, once considered inexhaustible, ran dry. In many towns, all that was left of the forests were "trees that were too crooked to be used except for firewood and seed."

As they had done elsewhere, logging companies either closed or moved on to where new timber could be found. By the mid-1920s, the Montreal River Lumber Company in Gile, the VanBuskirk Brothers Mill and Sandrock Mill of Oma, the Kimball Clark Mill at Kimball, and the Pripps Mill in Sherman all ceased operating and were dismantled and moved. Communities dependent on wood such as Kimball, VanBuskirk, Sandrock, and Emerson faded away with them.

Fortunately for many employed in woods work, the diversity of Iron county's resources offered alternatives. The burgeoning mining industry offered employment. Farms were being developed. The railroads and tote roads of the loggers, that had taken out so much timber wealth also brought a different type of resource, whose money and mobility could be capitalized upon--the tourist.

19

Saxon, 1897. The other legacy of the logging era was a land choked with stumps, weedy undergrowth, and tinder-dry piles of pine and hardwood slash. This was land nobody wanted. Abandoned, with property taxes left unpaid, by the same owners who made their wealth there, the Cutover burdened the county with lost tax revenue. Fires swept through regularly, with major blazes in 1910 and 1925. They destroyed any standing timber, seed trees, even the soil's thin covering of humus.

Hanneman Mill, Mercer, 1935. As the pine and hardwoods were logged off, sawmills had to diversify. In the late 1800s, E.H. Staples capitalized on the use of cedar for shingles. The mill's next owner, Dan Shea, started the Excelsior Mill to shred basswood, popple, birch and balsam into packing material. By 1935, the Cutover lands could yield only meager amounts of timber, but Walt Hanneman, who built his mill next to the original Staples and Shea operations, found a timber resource at the bottoms of rivers and lakes. By salvaging old submerged logs or "deadheads" left behind by the pioneers in nearby Echo Lake and from the Manitowish and Turtle Rivers at Lake of the Falls, he was able to cut up to 18,000 board feet per day. By 1946, this mill, too, had ceased operations.

Montreal Mine, undated. The daily work of the iron miner was long, hard and dangerous. The work day was not cut from ten to eight hours until 1912 and only then with help from a Congressional committee investigating the steel industry. Despite its hazards, work in the mines offered stable employment for some. Others combined part-time work in the mines with logging or farming.

Not all of the resource wealth lay above the ground. Before any human had arrived, geologic forces had created underground wealth that would be one of the greatest influences on the people of Iron county.

Nearly 1½ million years ago, sediments of slate and wavy beds of cherty iron carbonates were washed down upon the granite and greenstone bedrock that covered northern Iron county. Molten lava flowed over the land and down into great vertical cracks on the earth's surface creating "dikes." For a time, the land was submerged under a great glacial sea, and more layers of sandstone and conglomerate rock were deposited on top.

Then a catastrophe tilted this geologic layer cake, standing the rock layers almost vertically to a 65 degree angle to the northwest. At this steep pitch, the layers slipped apart, creating fault lines. Over the eons, rain water seeped into these cracks, slowly oxidizing the iron carbonate rock into a low phosphorus hematite, the highly-valued iron ore mineral.

The greatest concentration of ore was found at the intersection of a dike and the southern edge of the iron formation called the "footwall." At these points, the great iron mines of the Penokee Range would be developed.

Dr. Douglas Houghton, pioneer geologist of Lake Superior, suspected the mineral wealth of the area prior to 1845, describing it as "rock ribbed and mineral veined." So great were the magnetic anomalies of the land, that government surveyor William Burt in 1847 found his ordinary compass useless and was forced to plot the Wisconsin state line using his new invention, the solar compass.

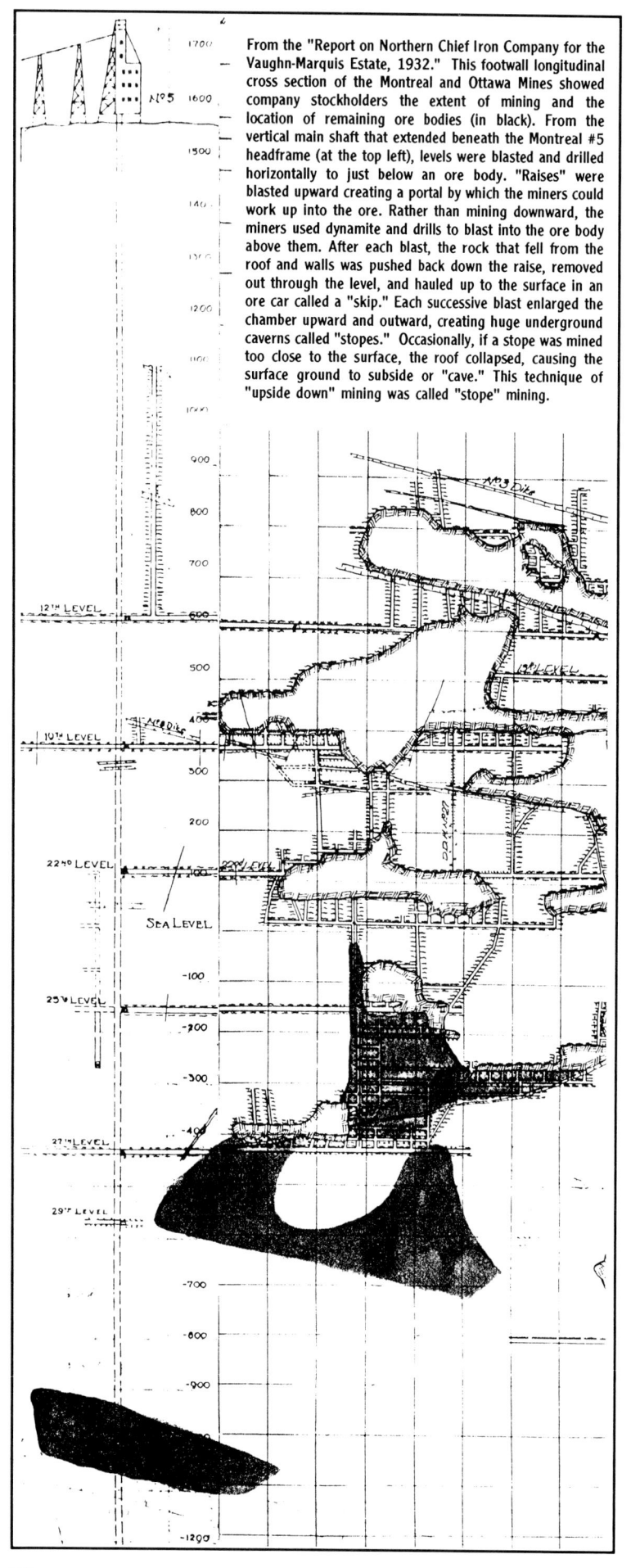

From the "Report on Northern Chief Iron Company for the Vaughn-Marquis Estate, 1932." This footwall longitudinal cross section of the Montreal and Ottawa Mines showed company stockholders the extent of mining and the location of remaining ore bodies (in black). From the vertical main shaft that extended beneath the Montreal #5 headframe (at the top left), levels were blasted and drilled horizontally to just below an ore body. "Raises" were blasted upward creating a portal by which the miners could work up into the ore. Rather than mining downward, the miners used dynamite and drills to blast into the ore body above them. After each blast, the rock that fell from the roof and walls was pushed back down the raise, removed out through the level, and hauled up to the surface in an ore car called a "skip." Each successive blast enlarged the chamber upward and outward, creating huge underground caverns called "stopes." Occasionally, if a stope was mined too close to the surface, the roof collapsed, causing the surface ground to subside or "cave." This technique of "upside down" mining was called "stope" mining.

Between 1847 and 1871, independent observations by government surveyors like D.D. Owen, Charles Whittlesey and A. Randall, as well as University geologists J.A. Latham of Wisconsin and T.B. Brooks and Raphael Pumpelly of Michigan, confirmed that the Penokee-Gogebic region possessed abundant mineral wealth.

The iron boom began with two discoveries made in 1879. It can and has been argued as to which of the two discoveries actually started **the** Iron Boom. On the west side of the Montreal River, representatives of the Lake Superior Ship Canal Railroad probed a tract of land and found a substantial volume of iron ore. On the other side of the river near Bessemer, a trapper named Richard Langford discovered chunks of red rock stuck in the roots of an overturned tree. Notice of the discoveries spread and attracted industrialists, speculators and just plain folks with picks and shovels who hoped to make iron the "red gold" of their future.

The Milwaukee Lake Shore and Western Railroad was so convinced that the Range was a good bet to capitalize on potential traffic in ore, freight, and passengers that in 1883 it changed the terminus of its new northern line from Ontonagon to Bessemer.

Many were willing to speculate on the Range's potential, but it was the Hayes Brothers, together with mineral explorer Nathaniel Moore of Ashland, who, in 1882, went beyond speculation. Convinced of the mineral wealth beneath a plot of ground west of the Montreal River called Germania Hill, they brought the county's first mining machinery, pump and boiler by train from Ashland to Mellen. Then, in 1884, they hauled the heavy equipment overland, to Hurley, using an oxcart hauled down trails that were laboriously cut by hand. It was a gamble, but on May 15, 1885 the first iron ore was mined from an open pit they called the Germania Mine.

In 1887, the bubble burst. Investors lost confidence, and the iron ore market declined, perhaps from confusion over the proliferation of mines on the Range. Many of the more speculative operations closed or would close by 1890.

Hurley, 1906. On July 13, 1885, only one year after the Hayes brothers had leased land on the west side of the Montreal River for mining exploration, the Germania Mine shipped 15 carloads of ore to the new ore docks at Ashland. Some consider this to be the first shipment of ore from the Penokee-Gogebic Range; others argue that a shipment from the Colby Mine in Bessemer preceded it. Germania's open pit ore was exhausted after 4,000 tons had been removed. Shafts were then sunk into "a magnificent ore body" below.

LIST OF IRON MINES IN 1887
(West from the Montreal River to Upson)

Hurley: Minnewawa, Germania, Little Colby;

Gile/Montreal: Nimikon, Bessemer, Kakagon, Superior, Ottawa, Odanah, Amazon, Opollo, Jupiter, Bourne, Moore, Trimble, Montreal, Father Hennipen, Lotta Option (later Vallance);

Pence: Pence, Snider, Old Nakomis, Emma, Union, Caledonia, Bullanty, Laura, Daisy, Ryan, St. Paul, Atlas, North Light, VanBuren, Cosmopolitan, Iron Belt, Atlantic, Vaughn, Iron Belt, Shores, Racine, Vaughn East, Annie.

The boom was on, and explorers flocked to the Range. Mining stocks rose in value and were often sold at high prices to enthusiastic, but unwary, buyers. Credulous and ignorant buyers were convinced that every forty acres of the Range held an iron bonanza that only needed the sinking of a shaft to open up the door of a treasure room. In 1885, there were three mining corporations offering capital stock; by 1886, there were 87. According to the Gogebic Iron Tribune, November 6, 1886: "Every day, new exploring camps are fitted out, and the woods are fairly alive with men all intent on striking it rich."

Gile, c. 1920. Looking at the Ottawa Mine #6 shaft in Gile from the Montreal #5 shaft tailings piles, this photo shows the surface view above the same extensively mined section of land that is diagrammed in cross section on page 22. The Cary Mine is in the distance. The mines represented a big investment by the mining company which benefited from the development of a stable community and workforce to support its industry. Communities or "locations" sprang up around the mines and with them a complement of retail businesses. Saloons, boarding houses, and general stores were usually the first community businesses.

Iron Belt, c. 1900. The Iron Belt, Atlantic and Shores Mines were important in the early development of Iron Belt. Since mining relies on an exhaustible resource, all mines eventually close either because the ore has been mined out or because market conditions are unfavorable. Iron Range operations were often threatened with shutdowns for these reasons. By 1901, the Iron Belt Mine seemed to run out of ore. Then the new #1 shaft bottomed out in deeper ore, and gave the mine a new lease on life. By 1913, the ore finally had played out at all three mines, ending Iron Belt's mining era.

In 1886, the Northern Chief Company gave leases to four different mining companies which operated the Superior, Bessemer, Kakagon, and Nimikon Mines. The properties consolidated in 1899 into the Cary-Windsor Mine or "Cary" Mine. Closing only briefly during the Depression, the Cary was electrified and new shafts were sunk to the 37th level, boosting production during the war years to a record shipment of 684,809 tons in 1955. But the deep hematite ores of the Range could not compete against taconite and high grade ore from other sources. Local people knew that when the great Montreal Mine closed in 1962, the Cary, to which it was connected at the 35th level, would soon follow. The end came on January 28, 1964. The Cary was the last survivor of the Penokee Range iron boom that started in 1885. It shipped 18,014,831 tons of ore over its lifetime and helped to build the Range.

Cary Mine, 1901. Mine tailings were dumped by hand in the early days of the Cary Mine. In 1886, the Northern Chief Company gave leases to four different mining companies for the Superior, Bessemer, Kakagon, and Nimikon Mines. The properties consolidated in 1899 into the Cary-Windsor Mine or "Cary" Mine. Closing only briefly during the Depression, the Cary was electrified and new shafts were sunk to the 37th level. Production increased during World War II and continued to rise to a record shipment of 684,809 tons in 1955. But the deep, expensive-to-mine hematite ores of the Range could not compete with taconite and high grade ore from other sources. Local people knew that when the great Montreal Mine closed in 1962, the Cary, to which it was connected at the 35th level, would soon follow. The end came on January 28, 1964. The Cary was the last survivor of the Penokee Range iron boom that started in 1885. It shipped 18,014,831 tons of ore over its lifetime and helped to build the Range.

▲ Old Montreal #3 Location, c. 1910. The man in the fedora in the middle of the three men at the top of the group is Dunbar Douglas, engineering assistant to Abeer, and later Superintendent of the Plummer Mine. Tony Chiapusio is the 5th man from the end of the front standing row. Matt Nibuka, shaft boss, is at the right end of the same row. With their hobnail boots, lunch pails, and soft hats outfitted with the new "duck" lamps that looked like a small coffee pot and burned grease or oil to produce light, these miners took a break to pose for a photo.

Montreal Mine, c. 1937. Overhead drilling in a large open stope at the 35th level.

Ashland, c. 1890. The first iron ore from the Penokee Range arrived by train from the Germania Mine to the Ashland ore docks in 1885. The Milwaukee Lake Shore and Western, later called the Chicago Northwestern, became the dominant railroad of the Range.

Ashland, 1888. Four-masted ore carrier boats await loading at the new Milwaukee Lake Shore and Western, Ashland's first ore dock. Transportation of iron ore from the mines to steel markets was critical to the economic success of the Range. With the completion of both the railroad from Hurley to Ashland and the construction of the deep water Ashland ore docks in 1885, the necessary links in a production chain were in place that could efficiently move ore mined on the Range by rail, then by ore boat, to smelting and manufacturing towns like Gary, Indiana.

▸ Montreal Mine, c.1937

(Lower right) Pence, 1985. One of the smaller mines on the Range, the Plummer operated in fits and starts from its beginning in 1904. It was mined down to level 8 and shipped approximately 170,000 tons of ore before it ceased operations in 1924. Shipping from its stockpiles of ore extended its life until 1932. The Plummer's 110-foot headframe is the last in existence in Wisconsin and still stands between the communities of Pence and Iron Belt, but for how long? Without protection, it is only a matter of time before this last remembrance of the iron ore days falls to vandals or neglect.

▾ The Montreal Mine prided itself on providing safe working conditions for its employees. Regular physical examinations were given to miners at the company clinic, including chest x-rays and joint, sinus, and circulatory check-ups. The clinic also provided chest x-rays to screen for tuberculosis among employees' family members, school children, and patients referred by the local health department. Records were not kept of the number of miners who suffered from silicosis, black lung, or other respiratory problems.

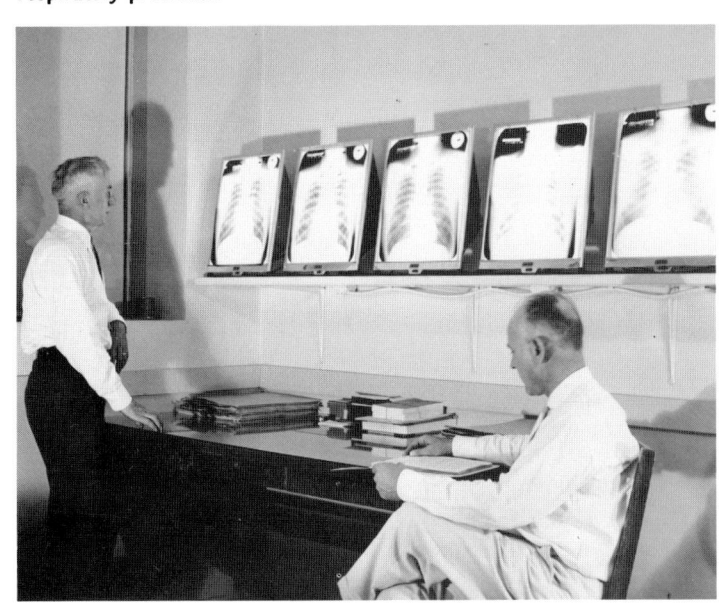

(Left) Montreal, 1962. Organized in 1884 and operated under the continuous management of the Oglebay Norton Company, the Montreal Mine was the "grand dame" of the Range. Known as the "deepest iron mine in the world," it represented not only mining, but the entire philosophy of the company mining town. When the end came, it came quickly. Amidst competition from other cheaper sources of iron ore, the Montreal announced it would close. On August 10, 1962 production stopped. In October 1963, milling and mining machinery was auctioned off to the highest bidder for $3,750,000. Within a year, the last ore was shipped from its massive stockpiles.

(Center) In May, 1964 the Montreal's headframe was torn down for scrap.

(Lower left) Hurley, 1965. Throughout the late 1960's, economic development groups, like the Iron county Area Resource Development Corporation, were established to attract new businesses to Iron county that would fill the gap left by the demise of mining. The mining companies sold their buildings for nominal amounts to development groups.

"Sheave Wheels,"
Leonard Kapenen, 1965

The sheave wheels have stopped turning, on the head frame of the mine,
No longer does the whistle blow to signal quitting time.
The dry house now is empty of clothes hung way up high,
No laughing, joking miners playing in the dry.
The water seeping in the drift is filling up the sump,
But no longer can you hear the rhythm of the pump.
The ore chutes are all rotten, the rails thin lines of rust,
There's just a ghostly silence, spider webs and dust.
The sheave wheels have been turning on the head frame of the mine
As long as I remember and before my time.
I often hurried to the mine when I was but a lad,
And watched the sheave wheels turning while bringing lunch to Dad.
Now twenty years I've labored, some miners twenty more,
And the sheave wheels keep on turning, bringing up the ore.
There are empty houses on the street where I once did play,
The fellows that you worked with have packed and gone away.
Now this is my sad story of a changing time,
The sheave wheels have stopped turning on the head frame of the mine.

DEDICATION TO THE FORGOTTEN

To those who gave their lives to mining the Range and
To those whose lives were taken

Over 750 miners died in accidents on the Michigan side of the Montreal River. Many more succumbed to the slow death of lung disease. The records of those who perished in the mines of Iron county were never compiled. It can only be surmised that iron mining here took a proportionate toll.

Saxon, 1930. Making hay at the Niemi farmstead. (l-r on the ground), Harold Niemi, Bucky Niemi, Nestor Niemi. While farms on the better growing sites in Saxon tended to be larger and more diversified, most cutover farms averaged 40 acres with about five acres in hay and clover, a kitchen garden, and tilled patches scattered among the stones and rough second growth timberland.

"Perhaps nowhere in the United States is there as large an area that produces as much pasturage as this cheap land in upper Wisconsin. [Here] there are yet large areas of cheap, unimproved land that is a desirable place to grow all the grains shown by the fact that yields of all the common farm crops are greater by five bushels to the acre than the average of the nation. These are Cutover lands. The cost of clearing is generally commensurate with the final value of the land"- reported by the Iron County News, September 27, 1913.

By the early 1900s, much of Iron county was "Cutover." The logging companies had moved west, leaving a wake of tax delinquent, stump-filled land that was drowning northern Wisconsin counties in a growing sea of red ink. Land could always be used for farming, or so it was believed, and there was plenty of it for the taking. There were also plenty of new immigrants to America. They could not own land in the old country and were eager to make their future on their own farms.

Many forces worked to bring settlers north. The railroads promoted farming since new settlers meant more traffic over the rails and a chance to sell off as their government-granted Cutover land. State institutions, such as the University of Wisconsin, were charged to promote and assist in the development of agriculture in the Cutover in order to produce a stable, tax-paying economy.

Not all the settlers came to Iron county to farm. Some came to work first in the mines or the woods, then moved to farms to live as they had in Europe. Mining or logging could supply a cash-paying job, but land newly-cleared, a cow in brushy pasture, crops of marsh hay, potatoes, and rutabagas, along with firewood cut from the land, gave the settler a sense of self-sufficiency and security shared only by people who know and love working their own land.

The transformation from miner to farmer was a slow, typically three-step process. It began with mining full time for the man of the family with wife and children clearing land, planting and tending livestock. Next came a part-time mix of mining and farming, followed by full-time farming for those lucky enough to find good land and had the skill to farm it and the tenacity to stay. While many tried to farm in the Cutover, few succeeded in establishing a paying operation--even with supplemental work off the farm.

In 1922, based on County Agent Dan Shaffer's program to test and cull cattle, Iron county became the 8th county in Wisconsin whose cattle herd was classified free of tuberculosis. The result was a higher quality and more marketable product.

Despite the optimistic reports, most of the available land for farming was chuck full of stumps and rocks that seemed to spring unendingly out of the thin topsoil. Stumps proved to be the worst obstacle. For example, roughly 8,000 pounds of dynamite were needed to blast the stumps from the Herman Crego farm in the Wall Street area of Saxon. Short growing seasons, typically less than 100 days, meant that many crops could not mature here. Markets were far away which added to shipping and production costs, making it harder for local farmers to compete and survive.

Counties in northern Wisconsin were the first in the state to contract with the University of Wisconsin-Extension for Agricultural Agents. They brought the knowledge of the land grant college to assist in the conversion of the Cutover to productive agricultural land for the economic benefit of the economically-strapped counties.

In 1922, Iron county hired its first "county agent," Dan Shaffer. His goal was to make "A Bigger and Better Agricultural Iron County." One of his first educational programs taught the safe use of cheap war surplus dynamite to blast stumps out of farm fields. The stumpland was the county agent's first classroom.

Culling scrub cattle, selecting purebred sires, improving soil fertility, marketing and other practical farm improvement programs were initiated. Many of them are still valid today. Agents used Farmers' Institutes, community fairs, picnics, letters, personal visits--any opportunity to give people information to improve rural life. While the county extension program started with agriculture, by 1951, it had expanded to include education for youth and homemakers. In the late 1960s, programs were added on community, economic and natural resource development, designed to build a strong foundation for all of Iron county's communities.

Hurley, 1895, the garden of Joseph LeFevre. Tobacco growing in downtown Hurley? This photo from the 1895 "Handbook for the Homeseeker" touted the diversity of crops that could be grown in Iron county--even a warm season crop like tobacco. Its purpose was to demonstrate the suitability of the county for agricultural production. Professor Goff of the University of Wisconsin-Madison poses with tall tobacco plants.

32

◄ (Clockwise from upper left on page 32) Dan Shaffer, Iron county's first "county agent," 1922. Although the work of the Extension agent has varied with the needs of the county, Shaffer summed it up in 1922, when he said, "to cooperate with every organization working for the agricultural or social advancement of the county, acting without favor, differences in opinion or political alliances."

Mercer, 1922. Extension field demonstrations evaluated the production of different types of crops including rye, soybeans, oats, peas, sudan grass, sunflowers, and root crops. They gave Iron county farmers valuable hands-on experience they could use to improve management skills and increase farm productivity.

Saxon, c. 1935. Farming soon depleted the fertility of the county's thin, acidic soils. Extension agents trained farmers to assess soil fertility and managed work-relief programs that excavated marl from marsh bottoms in the Saxon area. The lime-rich marl was an inexpensive soil amendment that enabled farmers to balance soil acidity and improve crop yields.

Given a good summer, even pumpkins and other so-called warm season crops, could provide a harvest that farmers could market to the growing number of tourists who visited the county over the years.

Saxon area, 1923. Programs–like this pruning demonstration–that helped farmers raise marketable crops of apples were part of the county agent's job.

Meadville, 1927. Extension demonstrations showed farmers how to use hot formaldehyde to protect potatoes from scab disease. Potatoes could do well in Iron county with its cool soils, short growing season and acid soils. They were an important crop to farmers from Mercer to Saxon and Gurney.

► (Clockwise from upper right Page 33) Gurney, 1934-35. (l-r) County Agent E.H. Dietz and farmer Bob Innes in alfalfa field. Improved soil fertility and new, more productive forages increased yields that translated into higher milk production and larger milk checks.

Gurney, 1935. The Joe Innes family farm is the only "Century Farm" in Iron county. Members of the Innes family have owned the farm for over 100 years. Since corn would not mature in the short Iron county growing season, silos were essential to farming here. Green ears and stalks were stored in the silo and fed to dairy animals in the winter.

Kimball, 1945. A combination of the old and new was demonstrated at the Hakala Farm. The ground-driven binder, originally designed for horses, is being pulled by the family's new workhorse, an Allis Chalmers tractor.

Kimball, 1990. The new Iron County Farmers Market location on the East Branch of the Montreal River was made possible by a grant of land from the Iron County Board of Supervisors. The pavilion was built by the cooperative efforts of volunteers, businesses and municipalities. It was dedicated to Lucy Luoma Hantula since her contribution made construction possible. (inset, l-r) John Sola, George Vallone.

FARMING IN IRON COUNTY

	1895	**1990**
Number of Farms	83	60
Number of Improved Acres	2,237	14,100
Value of Agricultural Products	$33,322	$1,765,000 (1989)
Production: Hay (tons)	495	9,100
Potatoes (bushels)	9,016	Not Listed
Beans & Peas (bushels)	60	Not Listed
Wheat (bushels)	29	Not Listed
Corn (bushels)	235	19,000
Oats (bushels	735	30,100
Livestock: Milk Cows	390	400
Horses & Mules	119	Not Listed
Cattle & Calves	191	1,600
Sheep & Lambs	18	100

Farming continues to be an important industry in Iron county, one that adds stability and diversity to its overall economy. The principal agricultural enterprise is the production of high quality forages for dairy farming.

In the late 1970s, recognizing the need to diversify agricultural production and encourage the use of idle land, a group of local farmers organized to develop a county farmers market on a sandlot at the corner of Business Highway 51 and 10th Avenue North in Hurley. Today the Iron County Farmers Market has grown to be the largest municipal farm market in northern Wisconsin encouraging the production and sales of high quality, locally grown product.

Turtle-Flambeau Flowage, April 4, 1925. Timber was cut within the boundaries of the reservoir prior to its flooding in 1925-26. The snags left underwater created excellent fish habitat while trees left standing in the water attracted wood ducks, osprey and eagles. The Chippewa and Flambeau Improvement Company built and managed the Flowage as a reservoir to store water for power generation downstream, so development has been limited to a few resorts, boat landings and rustic campsites. Although the product of human endeavor, the Turtle-Flambeau is as natural as the northern Wisconsin wilderness.

The pioneering days were coming to a close by the 1930s. The experience of the Cutover days showed that the resources of the county were not inexhaustible. However, with proper management, Iron's natural attributes could be conserved, even enhanced, to provide a variety of sustainable benefits.

Because of its potential for electrical power generation, one of the first resources to be managed was water. The Turtle River had already been dammed in several places to provide the quick flush of water to run white pine logs downstream. In 1926, its waters, together with those of the Manitowish River, were dammed by the Chippewa and Flambeau Improvement Company, to produce a "uniform flow" of water to generate power and make paper. The Turtle-Flambeau Flowage Dam created the 5.9 billion cubic foot capacity, 18,900 acre Turtle-Flambeau Flowage. A smaller dam, installed in 1912 to control the flow of Moose Creek into the Turtle River, created the Moose Lake Reservoir, part of the control system.

The flooding of the Turtle-Flambeau "drowned" nine natural lakes, sections of the Turtle and Manitowish Rivers, and what early explorers called "some of the worst tamarack swamps." What was once a swamp was now an expanse of clear water dotted with sandy islands.

The Flowage became a prime destination for fishermen and a tourist draw for both Springstead and Mercer. Family resorts sprang up along the limited amount of shoreline that was privately owned, the rest remained pristine and undeveloped. Legions of Girl Scouts, Boy Scouts and campers paddled its broad waters and secluded passageways in the 1950s, '60s and '70s. Many of these were city kids and the Flowage would be the first truly "wild" north country they had ever seen.

▲ Turtle-Flambeau Flowage, 1991. Calling it the "Crown Jewel of Northern Wisconsin," Wisconsin Governor Tommy Thompson designated the Turtle Flambeau Flowage a "special recreation" area after it was acquired by the State of Wisconsin from the Chippewa and Flambeau Improvement Company which sold it in 1990. It will be managed to perpetuate the natural character of its shoreline and preserve its scenic values and unique wildlife habitat. Its wild character will be preserved for future generations to enjoy.

◄ Turtle-Flambeau Flowage, 1982. (l-r) DNR Wildlife biologists Jeff Wilson and John Olson. Sometimes even Nature needs a little help. As the old "snag" trees that stood in the Flowage's bays began to fall down from the ravages of water and wind, favorite nesting sites of osprey high in their crooked limbs were lost. Natural nest trees were rapidly disappearing and with them the osprey. By 1978, there were only seven active osprey territories within the Flowage. A Department of Natural Resources nest habitat program installed artificial nest trees in hopes of convincing more breeding pairs to return to raise their young on the Flowage. Coupled with the positive effects of the 1972 ban on DDT, by 1990 the number of active osprey territories on the Flowage had increased to 22.

▲ Mercer, 1937. In the 1930s, public conservation programs were expanded with private efforts like the Mercer Fish Hatchery. Construction of the log-style hatchery began in 1935 at Lake of the Falls on the Turtle River, the site of the great spring walleye run. Mercer citizens, businesses, summer home owners, and Iron county donated labor and financing. A fish-rearing program was run cooperatively with the Wisconsin Conservation Department and finally deeded to the agency. From these first public-private partnerships, the custom of involving volunteers in conservation programs continues today in programs like creel sampling, hunter and snowmobile safety training, and lake water quality sampling.

▶ Gile Flowage, 1990. Modern resource management is a science. Techniques like fyke netting give DNR fish managers the population numbers they use to recommend size and bag limits that will protect fish populations, yet at the same time keep the anglers happy.

(Upper Left) T44N, R2E, Sections 25-26, 35-36, 1936. (l-r) John Morris, Iron county's first Forest Ranger, and Heino Hannula who directed section corner locating and timber estimating. One of the first tasks in establishing the new county forest reserve was to survey the land and mark its corners. Section corners were marked with pipes and brass caps. Large white wooden posts were placed on main highways and fire lanes where section lines crossed to indicate distance to the nearest corner.

(Above) Camp Upson, c. 1935. Civilian Conservation Corps workers from Camp Upson transplant over 300,000 spruce and pine seedlings from the County Nursery in Upson. This was the only county nursery of its kind in Wisconsin and made it possible to have on hand local forest stock needed to replant the Cutover.

(Left) Learning to plant trees, 1938. So that history will not repeat itself, a group of 4-H boys learn conservation and good forestry practices, demonstrating their tree-planting techniques to County Agent E.H. Dietz.

By 1930, Iron county began to feel the effects of deforestation and the tax delinquencies created, as cutover land was abandoned and left to go on the tax rolls. The unrestricted settlement of the Cutover land forced already hard-pressed local governments to extend services, like roads and schools, to more and more isolated settlers. As farms failed, most of these lands, suited for forestry not farming, landed right back on the rolls of tax delinquency. The scenario of farm failures, overcut timber, and soil erosion was being played out nationwide during the Depression of the 1930s. Against the backdrop of a new national emphasis toward conservation of natural resources, and with the assistance of County Agent E.H. Dietz, Iron county created a farsighted, bold plan to create a county forest reserve. The county acquired tax delinquent blocks of Cutover land and enrolled them under the new Forest Crop Law. Any land suited for agricultural purposes was exempted from acquisition.

The Tyler, Penokee, Island Lake, Mercoma ("Mercer-Oma"), and Knight Forests, five blocks totaling just over 80,000 acres, were established by resolution of the county board in 1932. On January 1, 1933, when the Wisconsin Conservation Department approved the first entry of these lands under the Forest Crop Law, the Iron County Forest was born. In 1935, two more units, the Caroline and Manitowish, would bring the county forest acreage to 110,000 acres.

A cornerstone of the plan was a zoning ordinance creating "Forestry and Recreation Districts"--restricted areas where "settlement is not permitted, but blocks of land are reserved for forestry". Adopted first by the county on March 8, 1934, amidst favorable public opinion, the measure was later ratified by each of the municipalities. By giving towns control over settlement it enabled them to control their expenditures.

The "land nobody wanted" was now everyone's land. Iron became the third county in Wisconsin to create the special forestry zones that would be the basis of today's county forest system. The problem of what to do with the Cutover had finally been solved.

MAP OF IRON COUNTY, WIS.

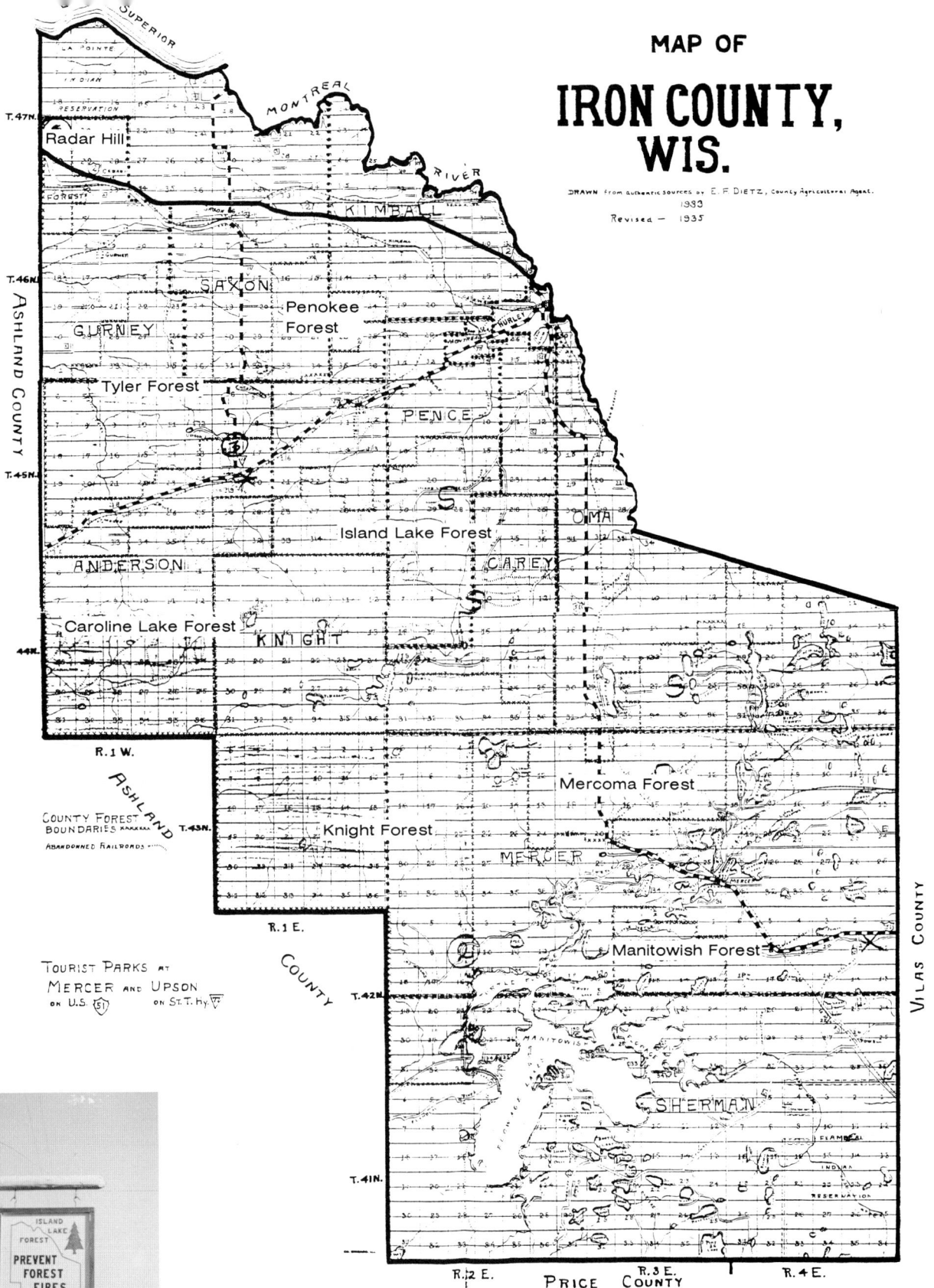

DRAWN from authentic sources by E. F. Dietz, County Agricultural Agent.
1933
Revised — 1935

COUNTY FOREST BOUNDARIES
ABANDONED RAILROADS

TOURIST PARKS AT MERCER and UPSON
on U.S. 51 on St. T. Hy.

▲ Iron County Forest Units, 1935. "Forestry will again become established as a land use high in value in times to come when the population has increased and the demand for timber has also increased. It's likely that the demand for food can be supplied by other parts of the country with a higher soil productivity than the upland stony soil of this northern Wisconsin county which is naturally a forest county." – E.H. Dietz, Iron County Extension Agent, 1936.

◄ Mercoma Forest, 1937. Forest fires were a constant danger in the Cutover, threatening to put up in smoke all of the work done to replant them. Reminders, like these signs placed at the boundaries of the county forest, warned the public of the danger. In 1935, the county received $290,000 for reforestation projects including an aggressive fire protection patrol and firefighting program.

(Above) Mercer, c. 1950. A network of towers located at Island Lake, Pine Lake, Radar Hill (later at Iron Belt), Springstead, Birch Hill, and Pleasant Lake provided fire surveillance. In the 1930s, the CCC and WCD employees manned the towers and fought fires. The only fire towers still in limited use are at Pine Lake and Springstead.

(Upper Left) Mercer, 1950, Frank Brunner. The first Smokey Bear costume in the United States was created by Frank Brunner, a Conservation Department employee at the Mercer Ranger Station. Frank made his first appearance as "Smokey" on September 28, 1950 at the Logging Congress Parade in Wausau. He got the idea to create the costume after carving a likeness of the "Smokey Bear" character from a cartoon featured in a 1944 national ad campaign for fire prevention. After seeing the carving in the Hurley Firemen's Parade, Forest Ranger Bernie Kluggin suggested making a costume so that a "real" Smokey could march in parades. Brunner worked with taxidermist Neil Long to create the suit out of real bear hides that were sewn by WCD office receptionist Ida Hart.

(Center Left) Another fire prevention character, "Torchy Timber Loss," was the creation of "Toots" Jaunti, a WCD employee at Upson in the 1950s. Torchy's biggest claim to fame was his adoption as the official Wisconsin Fire Control Logo.

(Left) Many devastating fires swept through Iron county In 1918, a fire burned from Island Lake to Big Muskie Lake in the Springstead Area. Mercer battled its largest fire in 1925 when 60 MPH winds ignited a blaze at Rice Lake and drove it toward town. Town chairman "Big" Ed Evenson ordered all men to fight the fire that burned 4,000 acres before it entered a swamp and died. Another large fire occurred in October 1947, said to have been started by a group of Iron Belt boys hunting grouse in the hills near Iron Belt. High winds, rough terrain, and lack of manpower hampered control efforts. Crews and equipment came from almost every town and high school to fight the fire. It took the first snowfall of the year to finally extinguish it.

▲ Mercer, c. 1965. E. H. Dietz's prediction in 1935 that the Iron County Forest would "eventually become a thing of major importance in the economic life of the people of this county... serving not only for the production of timber, but also for recreation of tourists and places for the propagation of game" has come true. Based on sound planning done years earlier, the County Forest grew to 171,883.14 acres and returned $254,732.67 in total gross timber sales in 1991. It includes five parks, a harbor on Lake Superior, 45 boat landings, 247 miles of snowmobile trails, over 150 miles of ATV trails, and 45 miles of cross country ski trails. The county's gamble back in the dark days of the Depression, to create a managed forest system from the Cutover lands nobody wanted, was an investment that will only pay back even more dividends in the future.

► West Branch of the Montreal River, 1986. (l-r, back) Rick Leinon, Curt Levra, Wanda Adamavich, (l-r, front) Roger Vokolek, Bill Trcka, Jim Vokolek; (not pictured), Crew leader Tom Popko. The Iron County Wisconsin Conservation Corps crew completes construction of a bridge over the west branch of the Montreal River. Modeled after the Civilian Conservation Corps, the WCC in partnership with the DNR and Iron county provides one year of full-time work for young people ages 18-25 in conservation projects.

41

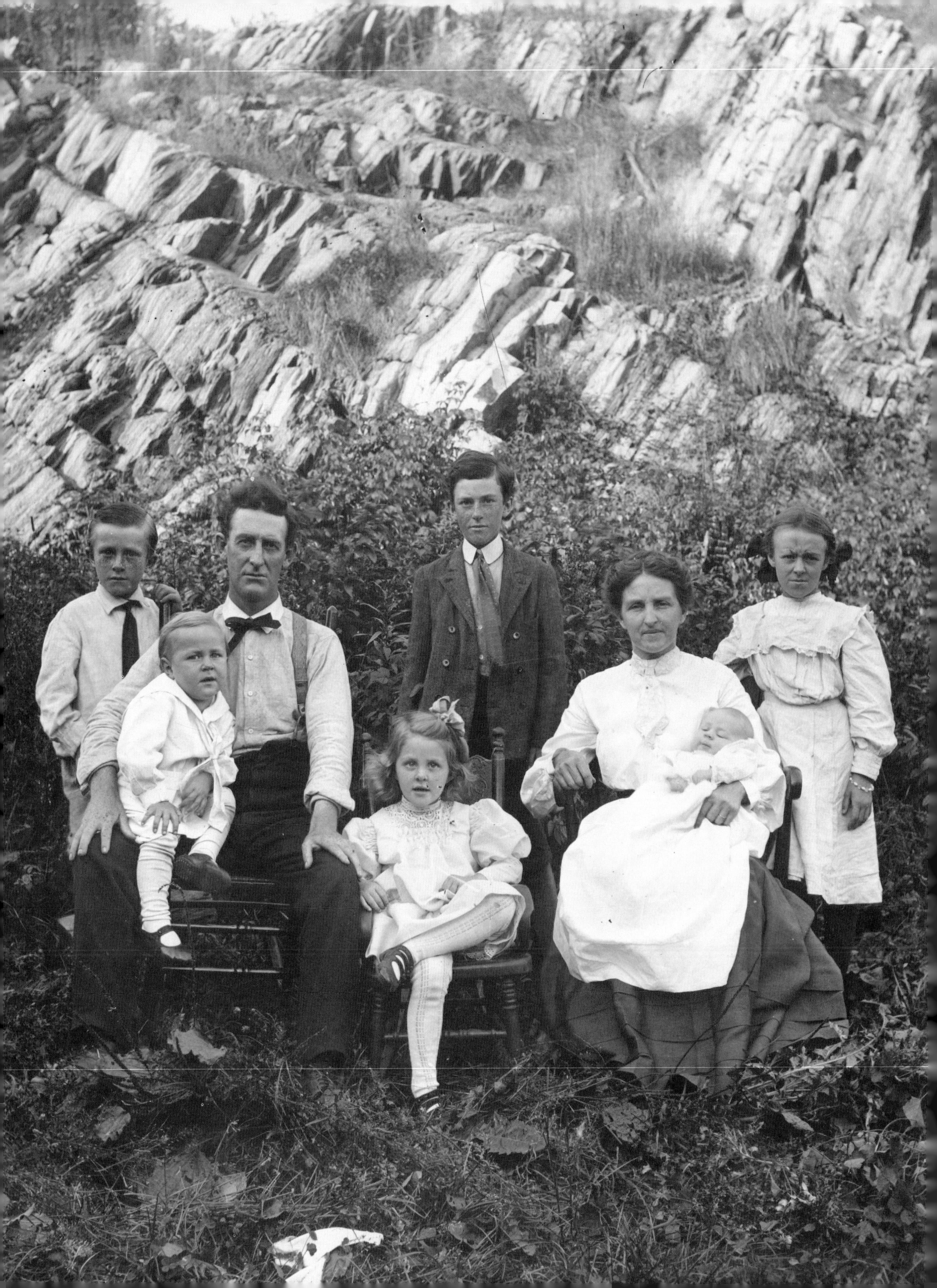

The People of the County

The Ojibwe or "Chippewa" were the first people to leave a record of their life in Iron county. There is no evidence of a permanent settlement, but it is known that the Indians hunted, fished, gathered wild rice and other edible plants in the county. They harvested birch bark and cedar for canoes, gathered the inner bark of the basswood for baskets and collected maple sugar at the ancient tribal sugar bush in Springstead for as long as can be remembered. Traveling and working in small bands, they ranged over the entire county, from Gurney in the northwest to Sherman in the southeast.

As part of the Northwest Territory, Iron county became part of the United States after the War of Independence. The French and British had been content to trade and had little interest in settling or displacing the native inhabitants, but the Americans wanted to put down roots in the new land. By 1854, the Chippewa had signed over most of their land to the Americans, retaining only traditional rights to hunt, fish, and gather in perpetuity throughout the ceded territory. With the Indians moved to reservations, the territory was open for settlement.

Some pioneers trickled into Iron county via the Flambeau Trail or the other rugged footpaths that led from railheads in Mellen or Bessemer. Others followed the waterways that penetrated the county from the north, west and south. Serious settlement, however, did not really begin until the railroads arrived in 1885.

The lure of Iron county was the hope of prosperity tendered by work in the mines or forests. There were at least two types of settlers. One group consisted of native-born older stock Americans, typically of English, Scot, or Irish descent. These pioneers, like John Burton of Hurley, had "Yankee" know-how and tended to be established business or professional people from central and southern Wisconsin. They recognized the mineral and timber wealth that Iron county possessed and had the personal resources to exploit it. As long as the resource wealth held out, they remained. The collapse of speculative mining in the Panic of 1887 and the exhaustion of white pine timber in the 1900s saw many of these pioneers return to their homes or move to new resource opportunities further west.

Hurley area, c. 1890. Their freckled faces and fair complexions mark this family as being of Irish descent. In 1890, there were more than 2,000 Cornish and Irish living on the Gogebic-Penokee Range.

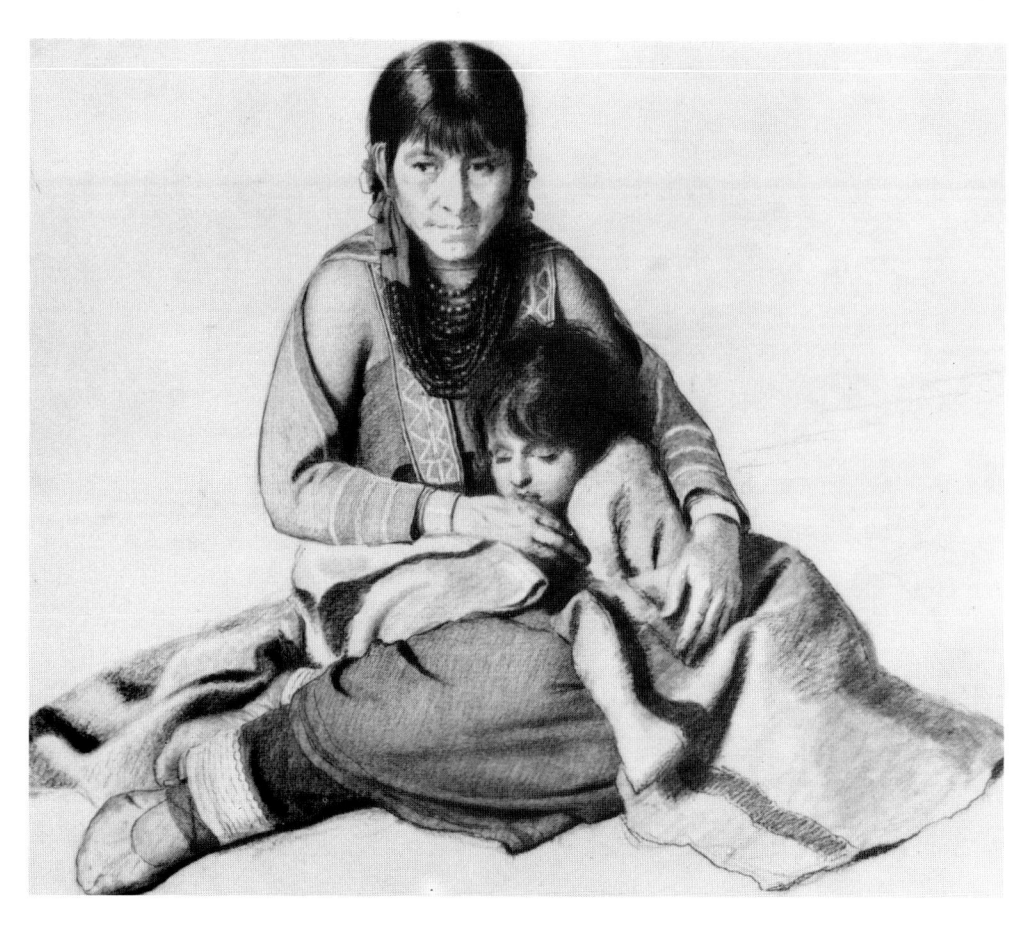

Unidentified Chippewa woman and child, c. 1857. Chippewa people like the woman and child depicted by pioneer artist Eastman Johnson inhabited Iron county in the years before the white settlement and afterwards as well. (Courtesy St. Louis County Historical Society, Duluth, Minnesota)

Other pioneer settlers, like Charlie Harper, George Schwartz, and Ed Davis, came to log and carved the community of Mercer from the wilderness. Bernard and Lulu Pripps, who settled in Springstead, also hailed from other parts of Wisconsin, but did not represent wealthy interests. These native-born Americans were a mix of nationalities including French-Canadian, German, and English. Distinctions between ethnic groups were less noticeable in southern Iron county than in the north, where a greater concentration of foreign-born immigrants settled.

The largest group of settlers were immigrants to America. They came to find their fortune in Iron county's mines and forests or to open retail businesses in the growing communities. The first wave of settlers--Cornish, Finnish, and Italian miners--did not come directly from far across the ocean, but from the neighboring mining districts of Marquette and Menominee, Michigan.

The Cornish, or "cousin jacks" as they were called, were among the first experienced miners to develop the newly discovered ore deposits. Their expertise gained them high-ranking positions as mining captains and section leaders. The Cornish "pasty" meat pie is one of the legacies left behind by these early settlers. The Irish followed the footsteps of the Cornish and, like them, tended to be more heavily represented in the upper levels of the mining hierarchy.

In 1900, Canadians were the largest group of foreign-born immigrants in the county, second only to the Finns. First to arrive were French Canadian pine loggers who took advantage of the Homestead Act of 1862, which allowed them to buy 160 acres for a nominal price if they promised to be good citizens and live and work the land for five years. Although their log cabin homesteads dotted the Springstead area, their true intention was never to homestead but to cut the white pine timber. They were loggers, neither farmers nor miners. When the timber was gone, they moved on. Irish Canadians took to work in the mines while the Scottish and English Canadians concentrated on establishing businesses.

It was difficult enough to move from one mining district to another, but, to immigrants from across the ocean, deciding where to settle in the vast new country of America must have been daunting. How did they choose Iron county? By word of mouth or, rather, words in print. Early settlers who moved here from the Michigan mining districts corresponded with family and friends, telling them of the jobs to be had on the Range. Foreign-language newspapers, that circulated in ethnic communities across the country, helped spread the word. Even employment agencies were used to advertise jobs and land in Iron county to readers in the old country.

The Finnish were the largest ethnic group to immigrate to Iron county, arriving in Montreal around 1887. The first Finns were miners who had left other Upper Peninsula mining districts. They tended to be Swedish-speaking Finns predominantly from the southwestern coast of Finland who had earlier immigrated from the old country. A second wave of settlers came directly from Finland, primarily from the agricultural provinces of Oulu and Vaasa in north-central Finland. By 1900, Finland's native sons and daughters made up 10 per cent of the county's population of 6600 people. Even though the Finns had been under oppressive Russian rule for 200 years, they proudly identified themselves as "Finnish."

The Finns were a highly literate people, nearly all of whom could read and write their native language. At one time, over 20 Finnish newspapers were distributed across the Penokee-Gogebic Range. They gave voice to the three predominant themes of Finnish life: labor, religion, and temperance. When they settled in isolated rural areas, Finns could more easily maintain old-country traditions. They could name their own communities--like Oma (Finnish for "our own")--and set up their own businesses and social organizations. As a rule, they did not establish their own schools. Finns preferred to send their children to public schools, where tradition was merged with new American ideas.

By 1914, there were several significant Finnish settlements in the county: Oma and parts of Carey along Highway 51; VanBuskirk; North Hurley; and the "Wall Street" area of Saxon. Many mining communities, like Iron Belt, also had significant concentrations of Finnish families where the Finnish language was and still is spoken.

Iron Belt, 1918. The Jack Nevala homestead on County Trunk E, near Weber Lake, was a typical Finnish farm. (l-r), Eileen, Ina, Grandma, Reino, and Grandpa Jack. "Bolstered by love, faith, hope, and a general amount of 'sisu', the Finns brought into the wasteland a one-room dwelling first, then a sauna, a barn, and a small clearing for hay and potatoes."

Hurley, c. 1901. The Oddino family was among the earliest Italian families to settle in Hurley. (l-r, front row) Mary Weber, Causin Weber, (l-r, middle row) Gene Darin, Grandmother Antonia Darin, Great-grandmother Martini, Anna Weber Pozzo, Angela Oddino, Ned Darin, (l-r, back row) Martin Darin, Cosante Martin, Benedict Oddino.

Most Finnish communities had at least one temperance society. Iron Belt had not one, but two, the **Valon Kipina** (organized 1895) and the **Valon Nousu** (organized 1898). Temperance societies were old country outgrowths of religious groups. They functioned as "alternative" social clubs, channeling the energies of the immigrants away from the temptations of the saloon and to more constructive forms of entertainment and social betterment.

Since many Finnish had learned about America from old country socialist leaders and newspapers popular in the early 1900s, it followed that many who came to Iron County brought their socialist traditions with them. In keeping with these philosophies, workers' societies were formed in several communities, like VanBuskirk's chapter of the Finnish Workers Federation. During the 1920s and 1930s, the ideal of gaining greater economic power from "strength through numbers" grew, and Finnish neighbors banded together to form retail cooperatives like the Iron Belt Cooperative Association. Today's Range Cooperative Services of Hurley, organized in 1931, had its roots as an organization of seven Finnish cooperatives that operated in Wisconsin and Michigan.

The first Italians, many of whom hailed from the Tirol area of northern Italy, followed the relocation pattern of moving to Iron county from the old mining districts to the east. Italian immigrants soon arrived from southern and central Italy, but they never outnumbered their northern countrymen. Although most Italians worked in the mines, a significant minority established businesses, saloons, and boarding houses in northern Iron County communities. The Italians established a good number of mutual aid societies, like the **Benevolente of Quattro Abruzzi**. Mining companies did not provide benefits to its workers. These fraternal groups helped immigrants secure insurance or at least provide for burial costs. Italian settlement in Hurley was so significant that an Italian newspaper, **La Nostra Terra** ("Our Land"), was published in Hurley from 1904-1913.

Unlike the rural-loving Finns, Italians preferred to settle in the larger towns or in mining locations. Like most immigrants, they liked to be near people who spoke their same language and shared their same customs. Many immigrants hailed from the same province, even the village, as their neighbors. Mining locations tended to be settled by Italian immigrants from the same old country province. The Cary location was heavily populated by miners and their families from the northern Italian province of Catarina. Nearby Germania was settled by Sicilians. Immigrants from the village of Capistrano in Abruzzi established a neighborhood along the Montreal River in Hurley. Pence was settled by Italians from the central provinces and from Corsica. By 1900, Italians made up the third largest ethnic group in Iron County, behind the Finns and Canadians. They were concentrated in the mining communities of northern Iron county.

Not all the Italians settled in cities or mining towns. One group settled in a rocky, secluded valley right in the heart of the predominantly Finnish town of Kimball. In 1907, a corporation called the Agricultural National League of Iron county, or **Agricola**, was formed by a group of established Italians in Hurley. Their idea was to form a corporate farm and lease land to new Italian immigrants who would work as tenant farmers. Although this was a common practice in the old country, the new arrivals had another dream: to own their own farm and home. The lease plan was abandoned, and the 28 forty-acre parcels owned by the corporation were sold to local Italians already living and working on the Range. Most of the new owners hailed from the farming districts near Piedmont, Venice, south to Campobello in Italy. They were eager for the opportunity to leave the mines to farm the logged-over valley surrounded by high hills which was so much like their homeland. As a tribute to their spirit of solidarity and their dream of a colony of Italian farmers, the area is still locally known as **Dago Valley**.

Other nationalities made up smaller percentages of the county's population. Swedish immigrants were one of the largest groups on the Range, but they tended to settle in Ironwood, Michigan. Norwegians were never as numerous as the Swedes, but they too came to work the woods and mines. Polish immigrants arrived by way of Ashland where there was a large settlement of Poles. Polish workers were often recruited by mining companies to replace striking workers or to ease labor shortages. Serbs, Croats, Slovenes and other slavic people also settled in northern Iron County to work the mines.

Immigrants of the Jewish faith from Eastern and Central Europe contributed to the diversity of ethnic groups that forged the county. German Jews, like the Heinemann Brothers, came from Wausau in the 1880's. They established one of Hurley's largest mercantile stores and played an important role in building the business community. Russian Jews arrived later and were among the most poverty stricken of immigrants. They also came by way of Ashland and started out as peddlers in the mining communities, but they were soon able to start small businesses. By 1895, Jewish merchants were doing business in every mining community in the county. At its height in 1920, Hurley's Jewish community numbered 300.

By 1920, the settlement of Iron county was basically complete. The county's population had grown to 10,261. The U.S. Census for that year listed no less than 35 discernible ethnic and racial groups living in Iron and Gogebic counties. It was a rich mix of people and cultures.

Iron county was a "young" county in 1900. Census figures showed that one-third of the county's 6,600 people were less than 20 years old. Twenty percent of these young people were considered "foreign born". This percentage is an approximation since many children of immigrant stock who were born here were counted as members of the "foreign born" immigrant group.

HURLEY and BARDON HOUSE LIVERY,

MORRIS & HARRINGTON, Proprietors.

FIRST-CLASS RIGS with or without drivers. | GOOD SADDLE HORSES for both Ladies and Gentlemen.

Terms Very REASONABLE. Office and Barn just west of Bardon House

HEARSE FURNISHED ON APPLICATION.

TELEPHONE, 42. HURLEY, WIS.

THE FIRST NATIONAL BANK

C
CAP
M
HURL
Will Cont
Boil
Orders for
MI

P.

Prescription Druggist

G. A. ALEXANDER
Justice of the Peace.

CONVEYANCING and COLLECTION
Promptly attended to.

AGENT U. S. EXPRESS CO

Offices on Silver Street.

turing Co.
RS OF
gines, Castings,
ing Supplies.
SPECIALTY.
WIS.

ANGE
wery
Prop'r.
EER.
ONSIN.

Spring Brewery

HURLEY STEAM BOILER WORKS,

THE NORTH-WESTERN LINE
Hunting AND Fishing Resorts OF
Northern Wisconsin and Michigan
REACHED BY THE
CHICAGO & NORTH-WESTERN RAILWAY.

Wagon Roads. — Trails.

SCALE OF MILES
0 1 2 3 4 5 6 7 8 9 10

Copyright, 1903, by Chicago & North-Western Ry. Co., Chicago, Ill.

DANCE TO DAN'S

BERTOGNOLI'S HALL, PENCE, WIS.

THURSDAY, JUNE 4TH

Hear JACK DALE, Al Jolson's only rival,, sing his latest hits.

GENTS 75c   LADIES FREE

Making a Living on Main Street

Main Streets developed at the crossroads of resources, transportation and people. Centers of commerce, government and social life, they truly deserved their title as the Main Street.

Early settlement patterns around logging camps, mining locations, rail stops or farming areas dictated where a community would develop. Some towns were platted by companies speculating on the future. The village of "Glen Hurley" was platted by the Northern Chief Iron Company in 1884 on the bet that the newly-discovered ore deposits nearby would be rich enough to support a community. It was a good bet. Other villages, like Magnetic Center, Pine Lake, Springdale, and Lockwood were planned by companies speculating in mineral wealth that was never found, and these communities were never developed.

The first businesses on Main Street usually consisted of a boarding house, general store, saloon, and post office. Boarding houses, unlike fancier hotels that catered to wealthy travelers, provided low-cost lodging and plain homecooked meals to the men who came to work in the woods and mines. If work was steady and the pay good, some would put down roots and establish a family in the new town. Saloons offered libations and a welcome social diversion for these work-weary men. They were not places for families or respectable women.

The general store was the real hub of the community. Everything was sold here, from homegrown vegetables to farm implements that could not be locally produced. A U.S. post office was often first located within the general store. Its addition on Main Street gave the community an "official" stamp of government recognition and access to important postal services like mail, money orders, and parcel post.

From this nucleus, the Main Street community grew, as long as the resources and jobs remained stable. With transportation, at best, limited to a horse and buggy over rough roads, most new settlers wanted to live close to work, church, schools and other people.

Manitowish, c. 1900. (l-r), H.J. Stone, Grandpa LaPorte, unknown, unknown, Horton Stone, Jr., unknown, Bernie Stone, and Levisa Stone. Manitowish grew on timber and the railroad. Pine was driven on the Manitowish River, but the arrival of the railroad in 1889 established Manitowish as a shipping point for timber. Businesses began to meet the needs of the loggers and settlers. In the mid-1930s, the Roddis Lumber Company operated a mill here and shipped out logs on the North Western Railroad.

▲ Upson, c. 1910. While the old Pioneer House, built in 1887, offered room and board to loggers and miners in Upson, the Turf Exchange-M.J. Saloon offered more "spirited" diversion which many of the men pictured here seem to be enjoying.

◄ Pence, c. 1910. Pence was built near the Pence Mine. Miners who lived in the town's boarding house, lumberjacks, or residents could find just about anything needed for the home or camp at the J.C. Eaver general merchandise store. Around 17 taverns lined Main Street. In one, the Mozenier Saloon, the disastrous fire of November 11, 1910 all but destroyed the business district. There was so much traffic over the Wisconsin Central Railroad between Hurley and Ashland, that a trestle was built in Pence to allow trains to pass over and under one another. It is visible in the distance, to the left of the man in the sleigh.

The second floor of Main Street buildings was used as office space for realtors, attorneys, doctors, dentists and oculists. Meeting halls were also commonly found upstairs. They were used by local government, traveling entertainers, sports enthusiasts, dancers and, most importantly, by fraternal and social organizations. In the days when people relied on each other for entertainment, halls were among the most important community gathering places.

The promise of wealth from the iron and timber resources of the county encouraged railroads to extend their lines into Iron county. Since the railroad was the lifeline that brought commerce to and from a community, its extension to a settlement made the difference in whether it developed into a thriving Main Street or faded into history. Such was the case of Ironton, a city planned at Saxon Harbor. The Lake Superior Mining and Smelting Company speculated that it would be the hub of the area's mining industry and the end point for a great rail line reaching north from Stevens Point. The Panic of 1857 and the discovery of iron ore on the Penokee Range to the east caused the Milwaukee, Lake Shore & Western Railroad to move its terminus to Ontonagon, Michigan. With no transportation link or nearby resources to support it, all that was ever built of Ironton were a few docks into the lake.

▲ Iron Belt (looking north), c. 1911. Main Street was the staging area for social events. Here, a parade of Italian organizations draws a crowd onto the town's wooden sidewalk. Iron Belt's Main Street originally ran north and south and the business district was larger than it is today. John Wiita's General Store, the Freteni Candy Store, the Iron Belt Athletic Club, the Hill General Store, and 9 saloons occupied the east side. Lining the west side was the post office, Peterson General Store, Iron Belt Opera House, Kyro Boarding House, Palmer Boarding House, Franzoi and Brighenti Candy Stores, several meat markets, and 7 more saloons.

▶ Saxon, Main Street, c. 1900. The J.J. Defer Store sold general merchandise to Saxon's farming and logging community. For those interested in other amenities, it also housed a theater and a restaurant.

▶ Mercer, c. 1910. Mercer's Main Street was moved from its original location along County Highway J to its present location around 1905. Mercer was an important rail stop for outgoing lumber and finished wood products and incoming workers and tourists.

▲ Hurley, looking west down Silver Street from 3rd and Silver, spring 1885. The depot is at the end of the street. The brick building at right will soon become the Iron Exchange Bank. The mining boom brought so many speculators to Hurley that "the solitary wilderness was turned into a beehive of activity." The interests of Hurley were in the hands of men of large means and determined enterprise who expected their village to be "the coming metropolis and center of this section." As the *Gogebic Iron Tribune* declared in 1889, "Looking back four years from 1889, Hurley consisted of one frame building, two log cabins, and one tent, and such a thing as a county division or any other division except the division of sleeping accommodations and grub was never thought of."

▼ Hurley, spring 1885. After walking from Iron River, Michigan to Hurley to strip earth at the Germania Mine in April 1885, a Mr. Swanson and friends found the much-discussed boom town of Hurley to be "a snake trail boasting only of four buildings along its entire length, those being the D.P. establishment, Mother Adams eating house, the Owls Nest, and the White Bear."

▲ Hurley, looking east from the depot (corner of 5th Ave. and Silver St.), 1887. Within one year from the start of construction, Hurley's Main Street showed remarkable progress. Commenting on the development of Hurley, the *Gogebic Iron Tribune* noted, "Each day, a new building goes up, and the woods resound with the crash of falling trees and the music of a saw and hammer." By 1887, Silver Street was packed with storefronts along its five blocks with many more businesses on side streets. On June 7, 1887, a fire that started in the Gogebic Meat and Provision Company destroyed all of Silver between 2nd and 3rd Avenues. A second, more disastrous fire started in the Alcazar Theater (the tallest building at right) on July 9. Most of Silver Street to the east and many of the buildings seen in this photo, including the Bon Ton and Caledonia Hotel, were consumed in the fire.

▼ Hurley, looking east from the corner of 5th Ave. and Silver Street, 1901. Hurley's Main Street was visited by a third fire in 1901. It started in the Klondike Theater, the very same building that housed the Alcazar Theater, where the big fire of July 9, 1887 began. Marble Hall (at far right) was built on the site of the Caledonia Hotel. The streetcar that ran from Montreal to Jessieville from 1892-1932 can be seen at the east end of the street.

53

Silver Street, Hurley, 1900

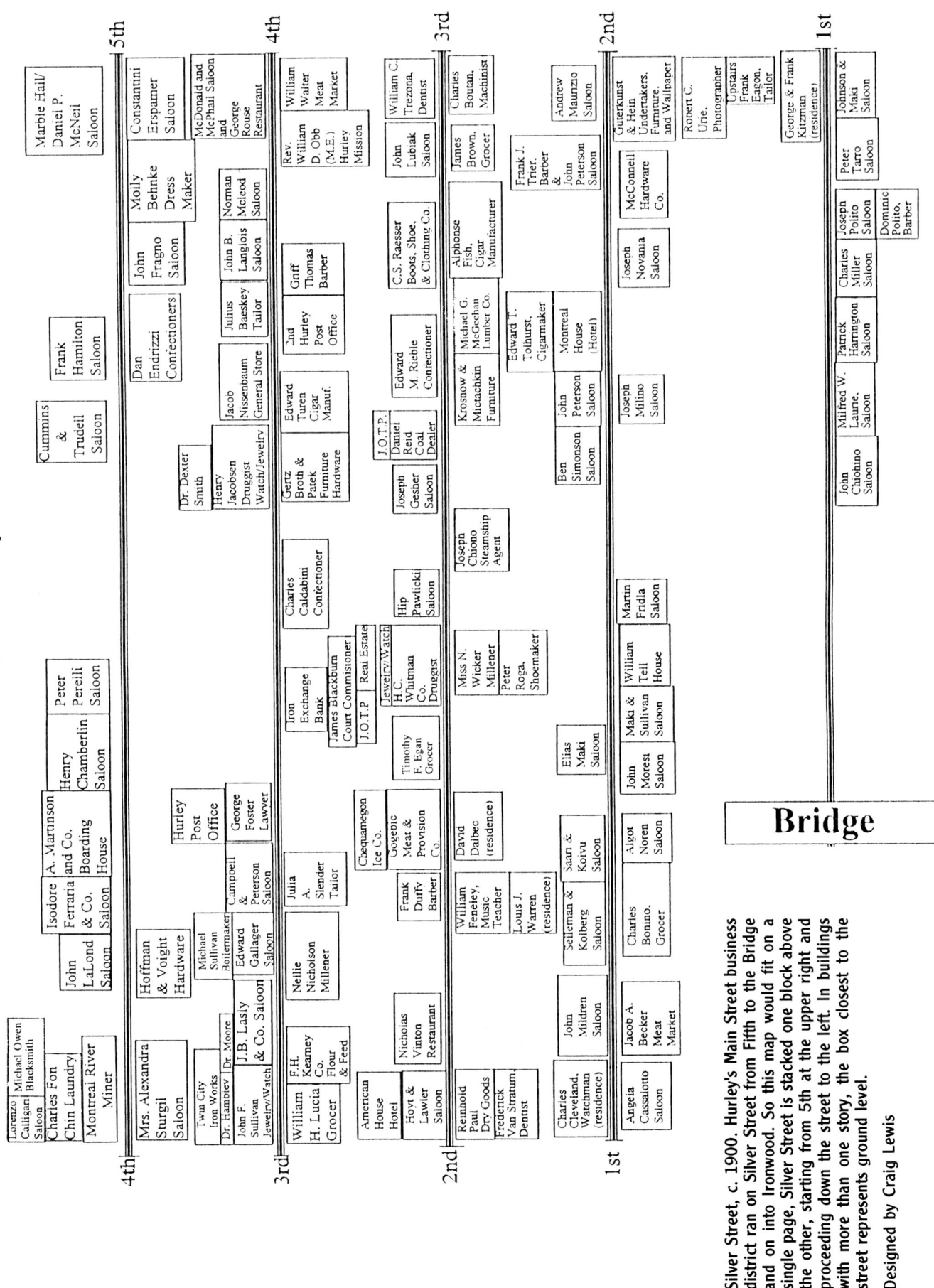

5th to 4th block

West side (left)	East side (right)
Marble Hall / Daniel P. McNeil Saloon	
	Cummins & Trudell Saloon
Constantini Erspamer Saloon	Frank Hamilton Saloon
McDonald and McPhail Saloon and George Rouse Restaurant	
Molly Behnke Dress Maker	Peter Perelli Saloon
John Fragno Saloon	Henry Chamberlin Saloon
Dan Endrizzi Confectioners	Isodore A. Marinson and Co. Boarding House / Ferraria & Co. Saloon
	John LaLond Saloon
	Mrs. Alexandra Sturgil Saloon
	Lorenzo Calligari Saloon / Michael Owen Blacksmith / Charles Fon Chin Laundry / Montreal River Miner

4th to 3rd block

West side	East side
William Walter Meat Market	
Norman Mcleod Saloon	
John B. Langlois Saloon	
Julius Baeskey Tailor	
Jacob Nissenbaum General Store	Hurley Post Office
Henry Jacobsen Druggist Watch/Jewelry	George Foster Lawyer
Dr. Dexter Smith	Campbell & Peterson Saloon
Rev. William D. Obb (M.E.) Hurley Mission	Edward Gallager Saloon
	Michael Sullivan Boilermaker
	Hoffman & Voight Hardware
	J.B. Lasly & Co. Saloon
	Dr. Moore / Dr. Handley / John F. Sullivan Jewelry/Watch / Twin City Iron Works

3rd to 2nd block

West side	East side
William C. Trezona Dentist	
John Lubnak Saloon	
Griff Thomas Barber	
2nd Hurley Post Office	
Edward Turen Cigar Manuf.	
Gertz Broth & Patek Furniture Hardware	
J.O.T.P. / Daniel Reid Coal Dealer	
Joseph Gester Saloon	Jewelry/Watch / J.O.T.P. / Real Estate
	H.C. Whitman Co. Druggist
Charles Caldabini Confectioner	James Blackburn Court Commisioner
	Iron Exchange Bank
Hip Pawwicki Saloon	Timothy F. Egan Grocer
	Julia A. Slender Tailor
	Nellie Nicholson Millener
	Frank Duffy Barber
	Chequamegon Ice Co. / Goyetic Meat & Provsion Co.
	Nicholas Vinton Restaurant
	F.H. Kearney Flour & Feed / William H. Lucia Grocer
	American House Hotel / Hoyt & Lawler Saloon

2nd to 1st block

West side	East side
Charles Boutan Machinist	
James Brown Grocer	
Alphonse Fish Cigar Manufacturer	
Michael G. McGeehan Lumber Co.	
Krosnow & Mictackin Furniture	
Edward T. Tolhurst, Cigarmaker	
Frank J. Trier Barber & John Peterson Saloon	Martin Frida Saloon
Montreal House (Hotel)	William Tell House
John Peterson Saloon	Miss N. Wicker Millener
Ben Simonson Saloon	Peter Roga, Shoemaker
	Joseph Chiono Steamship Agent
	Maki & Sullivan Saloon
	John Moresi Saloon
	Algot Noren Saloon
	Elias Maki Saloon
	Selleman & Kolberg Saloon
	Saari & Koivu Saloon
	Charles Bonino Grocer
	John Mildren Saloon
	Jacob A. Becker Meat Market
	Angela Cassalotto Saloon
	Charles Cleveland Watchman (residence)
	Rennold Paul Dry Goods / Frederck Van Stratum Dentist
	William Feneley Music Teacher / Louis J. Warren (residence)
	David Dalbec (residence)

1st to Bridge

West side	East side
Andrew Maurizio Saloon	
Guterkunst & Hein Undertakers, Furniture, and Wallpaper	
Robert C. Urie, Photographer	
Upstairs Frank Eagon, Tailor	
George & Frank Kitzman (residence)	
Johnson & Maki Saloon	McConnell Hardware Co.
Peter Tarro Saloon	Joseph Novania Saloon
Joseph Polito Saloon	Joseph Milino Saloon
Dominic Polito, Barber	
Charles Miller Saloon	
Patrick Harrington Saloon	
Milfred W. Laurie Saloon	
John Chiohino Saloon	

Bridge

Silver Street, c. 1900. Hurley's Main Street business district ran on Silver Street from Fifth to the Bridge and on into Ironwood. So this map would fit on a single page, Silver Street is stacked one block above the other, starting from 5th at the upper right and proceeding down the street to the left. In buildings with more than one story, the box closest to the street represents ground level.

Designed by Craig Lewis

Hurley, looking west at corner of 3rd Ave. and Silver Street, 1937. Fifty-two years after construction of Main Street began, Silver Street is no longer "flanked on the north by thick wilderness [with] Copper Street ....so thickly wooded, woodsmen would lose their way within a short distance of town limits." Paul's Store (right) was established by R. Paul in 1886, but was destroyed by the 1887 fire. It was moved to the corner and rebuilt of brick. (This is the same scene as shown at the top of page 52, only 52 years later.)

Downtown Hurley, looking east toward Ironwood from the corner of 3rd Avenue and Silver Street.

55

Map of DOWNTOWN MERCER 1900 - 1909

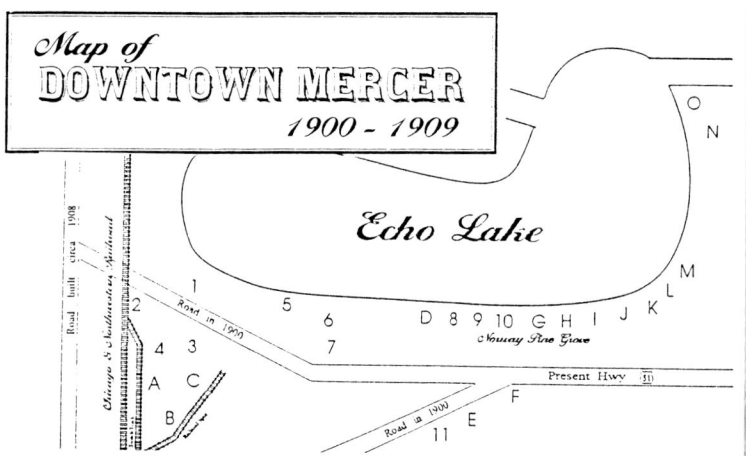

Legend

Existed in 1900
1. George Richardson Saloon
2. Chicago & Northwestern Depot
3. Hotel, Post Office, & Store
4. Store Warehouse
5. Sawmill
6. Blacksmith Shop
7. Louis Luffmark, Millwright (residence)
8. John Weber Saloon
9. Vaughn & McGinnis Saloon
10. Vaughn & McGinnis Boarding House
11. School house

Built between 1900 and 1909
- A R.E. Reed Blacksmith Shop
- B R.E. Reed Office
- C R.E. Reed Stable & Warehouse
- D Frank McGinnis Saloon
- G Charles Harper (residence)
- H William Hobbs (residence)
- I Joe Odgers (residence)
- J Joe Gonieux (alias, Billy Doe) (residence)
- K Tom Dowling (residence)
- L Tony Kraus, barber (residence)
- M Bray Back (residence)
- N Keewatin Senior Camp (older boys)
- O Keewatin Junior Camp (younger boys)
- P Dr. Hawley (residence) (not pictured)

◄ Downtown Mercer, c. 1900. Mercer's first Main Street businesses and railroad depot were located along today's County J, north of the present downtown area in the area known as "Pigtown." It was actually the nicest part of town, with wooden sidewalks that ran along a beautiful tree-lined boulevard to Main Street. The depot and Main Street were relocated to its present location around 1905.

(Upper Right) Mercer, c. 1905. This was the scene that greeted northbound railroad passengers into Mercer. The water tank and depot are at the center. The small building next to the bridge (at right) is a pumphouse that pumped water from the creek up to the water tower. Four passenger trains, two in each direction, and sometimes two freight trains rumbled through Mercer each day.

▼ Downtown Mercer, 1907. (l-r), Charlie Harper, his wife Ida, two children, and employee Bertha Brockman. Mercer pioneer Charlie Harper was considered one of the community's most aggressive entrepreneurs. He owned and operated several grocery stores, ran a cab service, and operated the Mercer Country Club. In 1907 he kept his general store–with restaurant and boarding house–open for business from 5 AM to 10 PM. He was involved in the logging business as well. Charlie, who liked guns, may have wished that he was a little less avid of a sportsman. He was shot in the leg by his deer hunting partner in 1908, which left him crippled for the rest of his life.

▲ Downtown Mercer, c. 1905. Another Mercer pioneer, Ed Evenson, with the help of George Davis, built the Mercer Hotel, strategically located across the tracks from the depot and in view of arriving visitors who needed lodging. The hotel was sold to Paddy Ryan and its name changed to the Jerome Hotel. Around 1910, Evenson built another tavern, which included a blacksmith shop, along Echo Lake. He also served as Mercer Town Chairman for 14 years.

▼ Downtown Mercer, c. 1930. Like many Main Street buildings, the upper level of the two-story building at right–the "Sweet Shop"– was a multi-purpose hall and community center. It was used as a town hall, movie theater, dance hall, basketball gym and, briefly, a Catholic church.

(Upper Left) Hurley, c. 1910, (l-r), John Reardon, Matt Connors, Florence Secor Pollock, Tim Egan, and Bill Detrick. The Egan and Reardon Grocery Store was built in the same spot as the old Germania Cash and Carry Grocery. Since there was no home refrigeration, most people shopped for groceries everyday. Some shoppers phoned in orders, and others preferred not to carry their groceries home themselves, so goods were delivered by wagon.
(Lower Left) Hurley, 1907. Hurley Bottling Works. Otto Kauppi (driver with blonde-haired boy). The soda water manufacturing business started in Hurley around 1887. Frederick Neibuhr, in partnership with Carl Lugviel, opened the Hurley Bottling Works in 1892 at 110 7th Avenue. Besides selling his own soft drink concoctions, Neibuhr peddled Waukesha Mineral Water and dabbled in copper exploration in Kimball. After a series of owners, Otto Kauppi bought the firm in 1906. "Huckleberry Finn" soft drinks were a popular company label.
(Sketch) Hurley, c. 1890. The Burton House, which opened in September 1886, was known as the "Hotel with 1,000 Windows." It was built in an L-shape with 100 feet of frontage on Copper Street and 80 feet on 5th Avenue. Inside, the traveler could find 53 sleeping

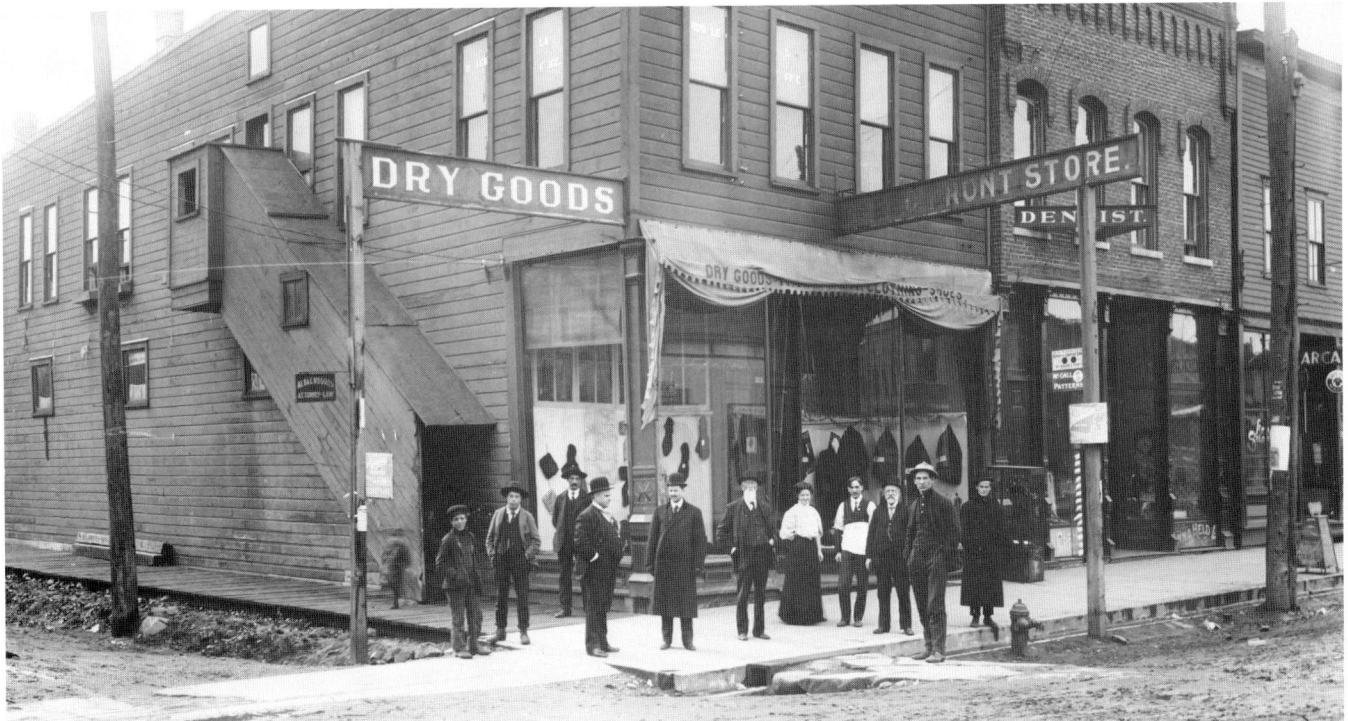

rooms, large double parlors, a light and airy dining room featuring exquisite meals; all rooms were tastefully appointed in beautiful wallpaper, wainscoting of ash, walnut, and oak, and hardwood floors. For the gentleman, the basement housed a bar, billiard room, and barber shop. Those who wished to enjoy the balmy northwoods air could promenade along the entire length of its 216-foot long, 12-foot wide veranda or just sit and watch the busy world of Hurley go by. Concerts were often played from the veranda by the Hurley City Band.

(Upper Right) Hurley c. 1910. Paul's Store, located on the northwest corner of Silver Street and 2nd Avenue, was a popular dry goods store on a busy corner. A policeman stood in the wooden kiosk in front of the store and directed traffic during rush hours. Standing left of the kiosk is Hurley Mayor Henry Mead.

(Lower Right) Hurley, c. 1910. Main Streets encouraged the development of businesses, each offering its own special services. The Red Front Store (southwest corner of 3rd Avenue and Silver) also sold dry goods, but specialized in men's apparel. Upstairs was the office of Alba Ruggles, Attorney at Law. The brick storefront next door housed a seamstress shop (where ladies could order a dress sewn from the popular patterns found in magazines), a cigar shop advertising "Anna Held" cigars, and a dentist's office upstairs.

▲ Hurley, c. 1900. (l-r), Dave Murray, A. Consie. Following the 1887 fire, the Voight and Homan Hardware Store was rebuilt to supply Hurley residents with items that were not produced locally–iron stoves, tools, hardware, cutlery, sporting goods, farm implements, paints, oils, and glass.

▼ Iron Belt, c. 1900. The Jackson & Wiita General Store opened in 1902 and was one of the largest mercantiles on the Range. After the first store burned down in 1913, a more fireproof brick building was erected. General merchandise and clothing were sold on the first floor, furniture and china on the second. In 1920, the partnership was dissolved, and the store became known as John Wiita & Company.

▶ The history of the Erspamer Store is the profile of a pioneer business person. Herman Erspamer came to Hurley from the iron mines in Vulcan, Michigan in 1886 with his family. When he was only 13 years old, he went to work for grocery store owner William Walter, delivering groceries as far as Pence. Work started at 6:00 AM daily and usually went as late as 9:00 PM. Erspamer Market, 1907. After eight years as a deliveryman, Herman Erspamer (in butcher apron with hands on hips) got the urge to own his own store. He bought an interest in the Becker Market and later became associated with Joe Martini's City Meat Market. His first grocery, located on the ground floor of Bonino's Hall, featured a butcher shop, canned goods, and staples.

▶ Erspamer's Market, 1915. (l-r), Ben Chartier, Fred Erspamer, Dick Erspamer, Herman Erspamer. The market moved from Bonino's Hall to the southwest corner of Granite Street and 5th Avenue in 1914. Erspamer's second store still supplied custom butchering. Several pieces of equipment were moved from the old store–the butcher's counter, Toledo scale, and the steer horns and poster on the back wall.

▼ Erspamer's Red and White Market, c. 1930. Still in the same store, Erspamer's Market saw some big changes since 1915. The butcher shop is still the featured department, but now a refrigerator case replaces hanging racks of meat. The archway opening on the right has been added to make more room for canned goods.

▲ Hurley, New Central Cafe, 1928, (l-r) Bill Allen, Frank Allen, Gus Lewis. Ham, eggs, and all the hot java you could drink cost only 50¢ at Lewis's and Allen's Cafe.

◄ Hurley, The Quick Cafe, 1920, (l-r) unidentified, Elizabeth Allen, Frank Allen, unidentified, unidentified. The Quick Cafe advertised that "our low prices grow smiles that never wear off."

◄ Powell, c. 1920. Mrs. Sherman's dining room offered visitors traveling through Powell on the North Western a good home-cooked meal and a welcome rest after the long train ride. At its peak, Powell's Main Street included Sherman's restaurant and lodging, a post office, and the depot.

▲ Hurley, The Q-P Saloon, 1900. (l-r) Tom McDonald, Dan McPhail. The Q-P was located on the southeast corner of 4th Avenue and Silver. It was several blocks away from Hurley's infamous lower block, but still well stocked with iced beer on tap and barrels of blackberry brandy, port wine, sherry, and several brands of rye whiskey including "Old 76 Medallion." In 1900, Hurley had over 50 saloons catering to boisterous lumberjacks and miners. Taverns provided a big share of the city's tax base in 1900, with each one paying $500 per year for a license.

▼ Hurley, 1954. In a town with many unusual saloons, the Museum Bar was perhaps the most distinctive. Besides serving the usual spirits, the tavern featured hundreds of wood carvings produced by August Jackson, who carved them with his penknife in exchange for room, board, booze, and smokes. Most of the carvings were social commentaries on life in America from the late 1800s through World War II.

▲ Mercer, Harry's Bar. Saloons played an important role in the life of a community. They offered a place where men could find refuge from the rigors of daily work and enjoy camaraderie with other men. They have been and continue to be an integral part of every Main Street in Iron county.

▼ Hurley, 1924. The Soetebier House, originally called "First Villa," was built expressly for the purpose of bootlegging. It featured three basements, one on top of the other, where booze could be hidden from federal revenue agents. The prohibition fortress had two-foot thick stone walls, topped with a green, glazed tile roof.

Mercer, c. 1920. Lee Gehr of Mercer predicted that the automobile would become an important new mode of transportation in bringing vacationers to Iron county, and he built his Standard Service station to capitalize on America's new mobility. He was right. Tourism has become the leading industry in Mercer and the county.

Flambeau Flowage, 1937. The automobile, together with improvements in highways, opened a new economic development opportunity: tourism. Vacationers could, with relative ease, drive to retreats like Al Koshak's resort to enjoy food, drink, and lodging on the new Turtle-Flambeau Flowage.

Chicago Sports Show, c. 1960s. To capture more tourist trade, representatives from Iron county began actively promoting tourism by attending sports shows in major Midwestern cities. The county's first official tourist brochure was printed in the late 1930s.

65

▼ Hurley, 1985. The building that once housed the Erspamer Market and then the Look-Up Workshop was torn down to make room for the Gateway Professional Building. It opened in 1992 as a medical center. To remain viable, Main Streets must recognize their historic importance yet be dynamic enough to adapt to the changing needs of the community.

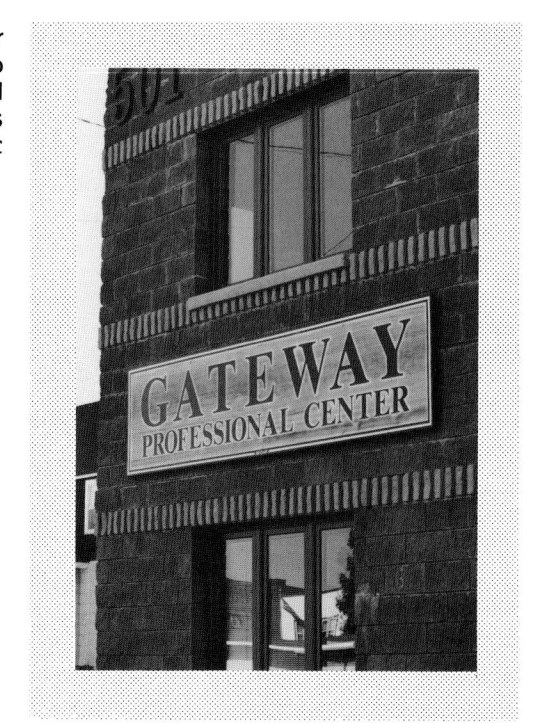

▲ Hurley, 1986. Some of Hurley's oldest buildings, now beyond repair, were demolished to make room for the expansion of a longtime Hurley business, Giovanoni's True Value Hardware. A downtown revitalization project that began in 1985 attracted more than $2 million in private investment on Hurley's Main Street.

▲ Hurley, 1965. An entire section of Hurley's infamous lower block taverns was razed to make room for the construction of Erspamer's Thrift Market, the fourth market operated by the Erspamer family in Hurley since 1907.

(Clockwise From Upper Left) The Iron Exchange Bank of Hurley, the Range's oldest bank, established in 1885, was purchased by F & M Banks in 1988, and Associated Banks in 1992; City Drug building received an attractive storefront renovation, 1984; Scandinavian Log Homes, one of the county's newest businesses, constructs custom-built log structures in Kimball, 1992; Action Flooring Systems, manufacturers of high quality hardwood floors, purchased the vacant Tri-State Homes factory in Mercer, 1988; Ave's Sport Center serves the motorized recreationalist and was voted #1 in service in the nation by Honda Automobiles; the Great Northern Motel, offering "hotel" accommodations and pool, opened in Mercer, 1990.

▲ Mercer, c. 1925. The world's largest fireplace, so credited in "Ripley's Believe It or Not," was built from native rock and timber at Whispering Pines Girls Camp.

▼ Dupont Road, Oma, c. 1980. Matt Annala found a great use for the abundant rocks on his Oma farm. A stonemason and carpenter, in 1917 he constructed this 60-foot high by 60-foot wide solid rock barn, believed to be the only one of its type in Wisconsin. The adjoining milk house and home were also crafted of massive stones. It is listed on the National Register of Historic Places.

Private residences were an important part of the community. Their location and architecture reflected the social status of their owners and their place on the economic ladder.

(Clockwise from Upper Left) Kimball, c. 1900. Matt Walli's first home was built from natural materials that were readily available. Now covered with siding, many original log homes built by rural settlers are still in use today.

Upson, c. 1900 (l-r) Mrs. Ed Brown, Phil Wolfe, Mrs. Jane Wolfe. The Phil Wolfe residence was typical of a plain but functional working-class family home.

Germania, c. 1900. The Alec Nelson home on Germania Hill offered room for a growing household.

Montreal, c. 1900. Richard Roberts worked as the Assistant Superintendent and Cashier for the Montreal Mine. His position as a middle manager meant that he could afford a larger, more ornate home, complete with a summer porch. This house was built on the old road to Pence, but was moved to Montreal.

Hurley c. 1900. One of the more ornate homes in town, the spacious Boyington House had a unique bay window, plus a summer porch and a decorated facade that indicated that its owners were people of means. The home was once owned by the Kimball family who founded the Kimball-Clark logging mill in Kimball.

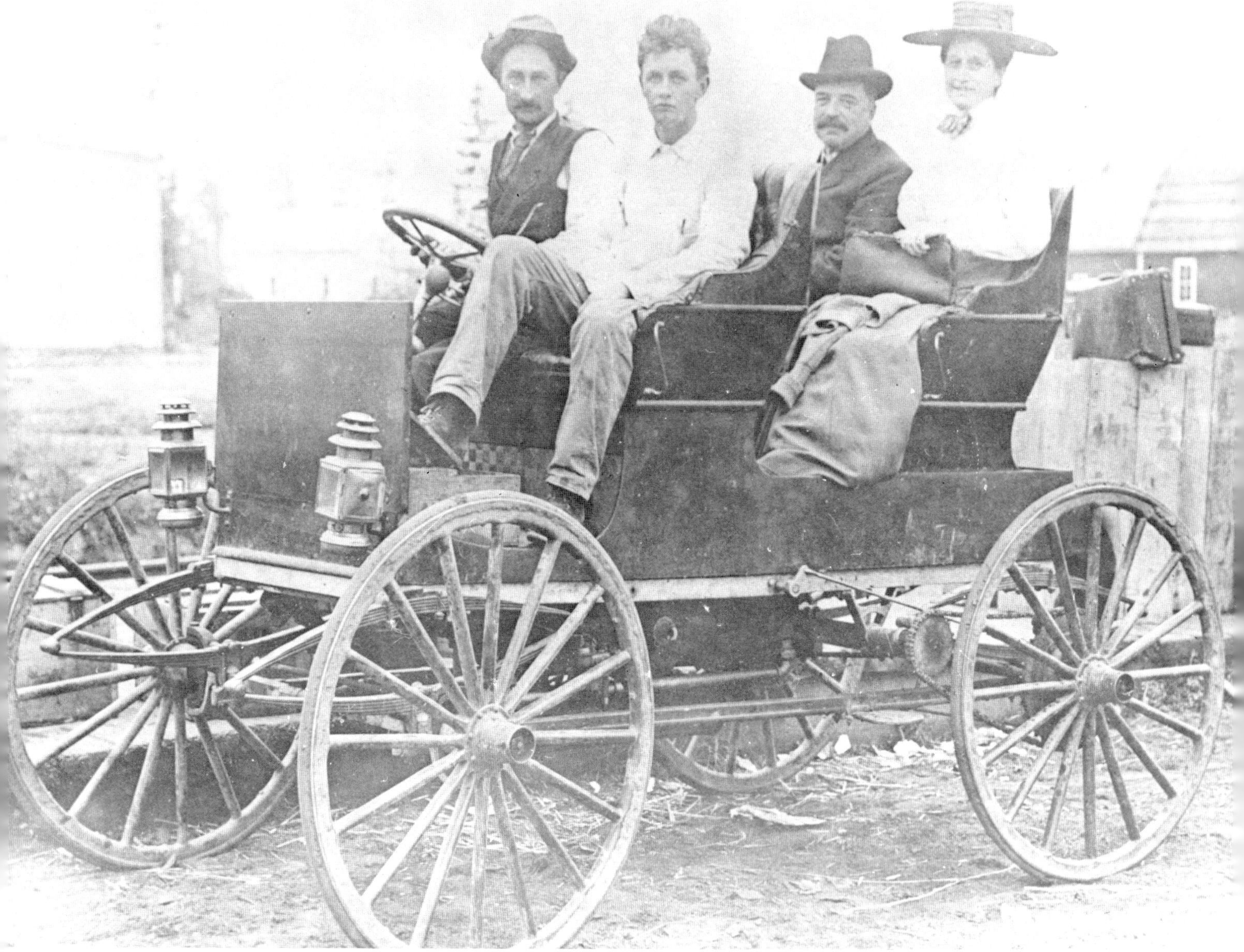

Moving People and Words

The development of Iron county began in earnest when the railroad arrived. By 1883, railroads flanked Iron county, but none had extended track into its dense forests. Routes into and out of the county were, at best, over rough trails, oxcart, or winter sleigh roads that extended from railheads in Fifield, Mellen, and Bessemer.

On the west, the Wisconsin Central line completed its connection north from Stevens Point to Ashland in 1877. On the east, the Milwaukee, Lake Shore and Western (MLS&W) reached Bessemer in 1883. The Colby Mine had just opened in Bessemer, and iron ore had been discovered near Hurley. A link to the iron range would increase freight and passenger traffic.

The MLS&W shrewdly set its sights on completing the critical transportation tie between the booming iron ore district and its new ore dock at Ashland. Ore would move on company rails, onto the company ore dock, then be loaded on Lake Superior ore boats for delivery to steel mills in Michigan and Indiana.

By October 1884, tracks were laid as far west as Hurley, but the railroad refused to acknowledge the existence of the community and only delivered passengers and freight as far as Bessemer. This changed in 1885 when the iron mining started at Germania Hill. The demand for freight and passenger service to Hurley was so great that the MLS&W not only stopped there, it had to put on a night crew to keep up with maintenance and track construction.

The first ore from the Germania Mine arrived at Ashland almost as soon as the docks were completed in the summer of 1885. That year, the Penokee Railroad completed the difficult connection from Mellen northeast, across the Penokee Gap, up and over the 1540-foot elevation at Upson. The Penokee become the second railroad to arrive at Hurley, but almost as soon as the connection was complete the line was bought out by the Wisconsin Central.

Mercer, 1904. Mercer businessman Charlie Harper owned the first automobile in Mercer. It wasn't just for pleasure, though. He used his new horseless carriage to deliver tourists who had arrived by train to camps and resorts around Mercer.

▲ Mercer, c. 1900. The Milwaukee Lake Shore and Western made a stop after crossing the Turtle River bridge. Tourists bound for the lake country resorts would get off at a small depot where they would be met by resort representatives. They continued their journey, by boat, up the Turtle River.

◀ Cary, c. 1892. Travel through the "Cary Stretch" was a lot faster and smoother by streetcar than over rough, dirt roads. The Hurley street railway system used excess electrical power generated for, but not used by, the mines. Streetcar service initially connected the west end of Cary to Jessieville, but later was extended to connect the principle mining locations from Bessemer to Montreal. In a sprawling area with limited roads, the streetcar was an important source of inter-city transportation. In 1892, it was estimated that a single car running between Hurley and Gile carried 1,100 people in a single day. The coming of the automobile sealed the fate of the streetcar. Service ended on October 1, 1932 at 12:03 AM.

▼ Hurley, c. 1900. "Number please"...is what early callers heard when they dialed the Hurley exchange. Telephone service made the world a little smaller, but its first use was for businesses, not residences. The relatively early establishment of telephone service in Hurley was necessary for the mining companies to communicate with each other and the outside world. George Roberts formed the Gogebic Telephone and Electric Exchange in Hurley. It was purchased by the Wisconsin Telephone Company in 1886. The switchboard was installed in the home of Mrs. Elliot, on 4th Avenue and Iron Street, but was moved to Ironwood in 1890. Around 1923, William Hoffman strung the wires fom Mercer's telephone system and connected the depot to the Chicago White Sox's summer house.

Also in 1885, a third railroad, the Duluth, South Shore and Atlantic, established a route across the northern tier of the county. Its tracks converged with those of the MLS&W at the community of Dogwood (Saxon). Both railroads agreed to install a cross-over track between their lines to guarantee transportation from Hurley to Ashland despite wrecks, floods or other mishaps. A union station was built to handle passengers and freight on both lines.

▲ Old Winchester Grade, Near Cedar Lake, c. 1905. Tourists could "hitch" a ride on the Mercer to Forestville (Presque Isle) lumber train. They would be picked up at designated points, like this one, by resort personnel. Conductors would stop the train at any place a passenger desired.

► Hurley, 1989. City workers installed a sign on a Soo Line railroad crossing in Hurley after the Soo/Wisconsin Central Line from Mellen to Hurley was abandoned. Competition from trucking lines and a decrease in freight shipped out of Iron and Gogebic Counties forced the abandonment after 102 years of service. By 1981, the North Western had abandoned the same line that had carried the first ore from the Germania Mine to the Ashland ore docks in 1885. The old railbed has been converted into the "Iron Horse" snowmobile/ATV trail.

▼ Hurley, 1992. It was necessary to flag down traffic to allow Engineer Ted Bueschel to bring this BXB railroad company locomotive across 5th Avenue in Hurley. Signal lights were no longer operational, and drivers were unaccustomed to watching for rail cars. The BXB Corporation leased the Hurley-Mellen tracks from the Wisconsin Central for a short line railroad. It could be history in the making, if freight and passengers once again use the railroad link to Iron county.

The MLS&W saw an untapped source of rail freight and passenger traffic in southern Iron county. In 1889, the company began work on a second line into Iron county from Lac du Flambeau north to Mercer, then on to Hurley. The first train arrived in Mercer in 1894.

By the summer of 1889, four MLS&W passenger trains, and two Wisconsin Central trains arrived in Hurley everyday. The railroad continued to be the area's lifeline, bringing in new settlers, business, and supplies until the age of the automobile.

73

▲ Hurley, c. 1960. The construction of the Highway 51 interchange improved access into Hurley and Iron county via US 2. In 1912, there were only nine autos in Iron county; by 1922, the number had increased to 580. Local governments in Iron county were constantly lobbied by citizens and businesses to improve roads. It was not until 1933 that the northern half of "Old Highway 10," from the Ashland County line to Hurley and Mercer, was replaced by the concrete-paved US 2.

◄ Mercer, 1923 (l-r), Bill Ahlgrim, Ernie Ahlgrim. Instead of a bridge, this inexpensive plank road was built over low spots in the road near Mercer. It took two days to make a trip by car from Chicago to Mercer. Obtaining gas and tires was a challenge, as was navigating without maps or road signs.

▼ Mercer, c. 1920. The airport at Whispering Pines Girls Camp may have been the county's first landing field, but its days were short lived. The camp was closed and the field planted to pine by Keith Jesse. On December 1, 1949, the first commercial airline and airmail service to Iron and Gogebic counties began with the arrival of a Wisconsin Central Airlines flight into the new Gogebic-Iron Airport in Ironwood Township.

▲ Ironwood, 1955. WJMS-AM Radio broke the airwaves in November 1931, bringing news, snappy tunes, colorful radio personalities, and old-time radio shows into homes in Iron and Gogebic counties. The Ironwood-based station added an FM format in 1974. Iron county's only licensed radio station, WHRY-AM (for HURLEY) went on the air in May 1985, and is operated in Ironwood as a sister station to station WUPM-FM.

▶ Hurley, 1990. The *Iron County Miner* installs a new sign, dedicating its establishment. Before the days of radio and television, the newspaper was the most important news medium. The *Montreal River Miner* (established in 1885) eventually took over the operations of all the competing community papers including the *Gogebic Iron Tribune* (1886-1893), *Iron County Republican* (1894-1903), *La Nostra Terra* (1904-1913), and the *Iron County News* (1913-1950). In 1950 its name was changed to the *Iron County Miner*. The goal of all the papers was summed up in the first issue of the *Montreal River Miner*, October 8, 1885: "We, today, present the people of this mining region with the first newspaper ever printed on the range. It will be independent in and of politics and thus be in the position to praise or condemn where damnation appears more appropriate...Without making further promises- we take our bow."

75

76

City and County Schools

"Schools must do more than develop fine bodies and minds; they must develop character." --J.E. Murphy, Superintendent of the Hurley Schools (1908-1955)

Iron county families knew their children were their most important resource and they wanted a better life for them. A good education was the basis of this dream. County residents have always shown strong support for learning. A strong public education system was developed, supplemented by church schools and non-traditional classroom learning.

The school was the focal point of every community. Usually one of the first buildings constructed, it often doubled as the town hall and a religious meeting place. Among the first public schools organized were Hurley (1886), Kimball (1886), Knight's Blue School (1890), Mercer's Green School (1894), Saxon (around 1897), and Manitowish (1898). In 1895, the county's first superintendent of schools, Miss Kathleen Nicholson, was hired to manage the growing rural school system. By 1900, nearly all the county's communities had at least one public school offering lessons through the eighth grade and open to students from age 4 to 20.

Religious and special schools sprang up in the 1890s in Hurley. Father Gilbert started a Catholic school. A Lutheran school, headed by a German teacher, taught students the language of the old country. Miss Summers started the first night classes and offered instruction in writing. Mrs. Hayes Chenoweth, whose sons founded the Germania Mine, started the first adult education school for miners. It included a library and a literary society, and featured weekly debates.

While attendance was compulsory to age 14, many students did not continue their schooling beyond the eighth grade. Boys and girls could go to work--legally--at age 14 and--illegally--at a younger age, and the financial situation often required them to do so. On family farms everyone worked--men, women, boys, girls, grandpa and grandma. Young men could find work in logging camps, sawmills, mines, and on Main Street. For the

Hurley, 1897. (l-r) Amelia Reible, Leola Luby, Bessie Jewell, and Frank Husen. The Hurley High School graduating class of 1897 dressed in their finest for their graduation picture. Not all young people, especially young men, had the need or opportunity to go on to high school. Graduation was a big event in a young person's life.

Springstead, c. 1910. (l-r, front row) Iva Hall, Ruth Hall, Ruth Brown, Norman Pripps, (l-r, back row) Mae Hall, Lucille Ablie (teacher), Nellie Hall, Lois Brown. Early school settings were rustic. Springstead's first school, the Maggie May School, started by Bernhard Pripps in 1910, was held in an old French Canadian logger's cabin.

VanBuskirk, c. 1900. (l-r) Lydia Hendrickson, Rauha Koski, Ina Anderson, Jennue Bentilla, Mayme Rein, Lena Hendrickson, Tillie Hannula, Jennie Rokola, Carl Lorraine, John Kalliomaa, Otto Jacobson, Fred Hannula, Elias Niemi, Eino Hendrickson, Ted Thompson, Andrew Krall, Alex Niemi, and Verner Hendrickson. The teacher was Charity Davis. The Central School was a focal point in Oma's early history. It was located on what is now County C until it 1906, when it burned down.

average young woman, the economic outlook was less promising. A girl could cook and clean for a middle class or a wealthy family. She might also work as clerk in a store, or take up dress or hat making. She could also become a teacher. A high school diploma was all the credential that a young woman needed to move from the student's desk to the teacher's spot at a country school. Once hired by a local district, a teacher was expected to continue her education at summer teachers' institutes or at one of Wisconsin's teacher training or "normal" schools. No matter what job she held, a woman was expected to marry and make her home and family her career.

The first graduating class of the Hurley Free High School, on June 9, 1893 consisted totally of young women: Laura Duffy, Anna Louis, Henrietta Whiteside, Edith Newell, Caddie McLarty, and Julia Reible. The essays they presented as part of their graduation ceremony covered subjects that would be appropriate a century later: "Avenues Open to Women" and "The Value of Education." Their class motto, "Perseverance Wins Success," may reflect their appreciation of the commitment required of them as women in the working world.

As more settlers arrived, put down roots, and had families, the number of school children grew well beyond the capacity of the old one-room school. In 1920, the county's population peaked at 10,261. There were 14 one-room rural schools, two second-class state-graded schools, two first-class state-graded schools, six ward schools, and four high schools, some with grades below. St. Mary's in Hurley was the county's only parochial school. All these schools seemed to be working. By 1930, illiteracy rates in the county had dropped from 10 per cent in 1920 to 4.8 per cent.

▸ Montreal, 1907. Conditions were getting a little crowded at the old Montreal wooden school in 1907. As the need for larger and more functional classroom space increased, communities taxed themselves to build wooden schools and sometimes larger brick schools. In the 1930s, the county's population began to drop. Communities faced the problems of declining enrollments and fewer taxpayers to support their aging schools. The state encouraged the closing of smaller country schools and the busing of students to larger facilities where they could be exposed to broader experiences. School consolidation, like the merger of the Iron Belt School in 1957 into Hurley Joint District #1, was generally accepted by most voters who saw it as a way to benefit from the economies of scale and still provide a good education for their children. The closing of the local school was not without sadness for those who had looked to it as a center of activity and a source of pride. By 1993, only two school districts and two school buildings were operating in Iron county: the Hurley K-12, in the north and the Mercer K-12 in the south.

(Center) Hinkle, c. 1941. The Hinkle horse-drawn school bus offered students returning from the Hurley school a ride home from US 2, where the Bertoluzza motor bus dropped them off. William Johnson drove the wood-heated bus after town roads became snow covered and the motorized bus could no longer make the 1½ mile trip from the highway to the Hinkle School area. In the spring, the town contracted with the county blower to cut through accumulations of snow, often three to four feet thick. The teamster would swap the sleigh for a wagon made from the chassis and wheels of a large auto and resume the route until the danger of frost heaves and mud holes passed.

▾ Mercer, 1938. The Mercer School has always been at the heart of the community. The first school, called the "Old Green School" (the second building at right), was started by pioneer educator Charles Moffat in 1894. Its teaching staff consisted of Miss Fanny Folsum and Miss Anne Weber, who some called the "Belle of Mercer." In 1912, Mercer organized School District #1 and built the red brick school (at left) to house grades K-12. The old wooden school was used briefly for the 7th or 8th grades, until it was converted into a hot lunch cafeteria by the Hassenburg family. In 1959, a separate kindergarten was formed. Logs from the Hanneman Mill were piled across the street from the school. On the far right of the photo, stands the log Mercer Community Building.

79

▲ Gurney, 1952. The 1951-52 graduating class of Gurney School grades 1-8. (l-r, front row), Kathy Younger, Larry Jarvela, Bonnie Jarvela, Cheryl Lauren, (l-r, second row) ____ Halvorson, Janice Rowe, Besty Younger, Bonnie Innes, Donna Younger, Peggy Jarvela, Bonny Lauren, (l-r, third row) Roger Adamavich, Wayne Hoffman, Robert Innes, Grace Hardie, ____ Halvorsen, Earl Innes, Lois Younger, (l-r, back row) Robert Rowe, Jane Heffner, Nancy Heffner, John Innes, George Innes, Lane Martinka, Donald Heffner. Teachers (extreme left) Miss Bierl, (extreme right) Mrs. Magnusun. The Gurney School operated until 1964 when it was consolidated into the Hurley School.

◄ Mercer, 1992. A modern classroom in the new Mercer School addition. Two important school referendums were placed before the voters in 1988 and 1991 that would set the future of education in Iron county for years to come. While other school districts in Wisconsin could not pass school consolidation or improvement referendums, voters in the Hurley School District in 1988 overwhelmingly approved funding to construct a new Hurley K-12 School to replace the aging J.E. Murphy School and consolidate the remaining Roosevelt and South Side Schools. Voters in Mercer showed the same strong level of support for education in 1991 when they voted to close the aging red brick school, attached to the high school, and built a new school wing for grades K-8.

▸ Meadville, 1927. 4-H was originally developed as an outgrowth of University of Wisconsin-Extension educational programs for rural families. "Boys and Girls Club" work, the predecessor to 4-H, began as early as 1923 in Iron county. As agent Dan Shaffer said, "We must have a place for the boy and girl in our agricultural program. The boy and girl is the man and woman of tomorrow. We must help them to take over the reins when the time comes, and there is no better way than Boys and Girls Clubs."

(Center) Mercer, 1952. Mercer 4-H'ers exhibited their float in the 4th of July parade. During World War II, 4-H activities were conducted by both the Agriculture Agent and the War Food Agent. After the 1950's, 4-H work became a part-time responsibility of one of the county extension agents. It was not until 1990 that Iron county hired a full-time 4-H Agent.

▾ Ironwood, 1992. Iron county 4-H youth and leaders take a break from operating their recycling center located in Ironwood. (l-r, front row) Jeremy Walston, Joe Sargent, Anna Holm, Justin Zanella, John Swartz (l-r, back row) Judy Atchison-4-H Leader, Shawn Clemens, Joe Atchison, Jon Holm, Jeri Luoma, Jean Barto, Randy Kirchhoff-4-H Leader, Deb Swartz-4-H Leader, Jillian Kirchhoff-4-H Agent, and Kaitlin Kirchhoff (in backpack). Not all learning takes place inside the classroom. A "hands on" experience to teach Mercer 4-H youth about recycling expanded to include 4-H'ers from the Hurley and Saxon areas. The youth formed the Iron County 4-H Recycling Cooperative and operated two recycling centers, in Mercer and Ironwood. The 4-H project not only taught the youth the importance of recycling to the environment and business skills, but it also was the first recycling program in Iron county and helped lead the way to the development of the county's own recycling program.

81

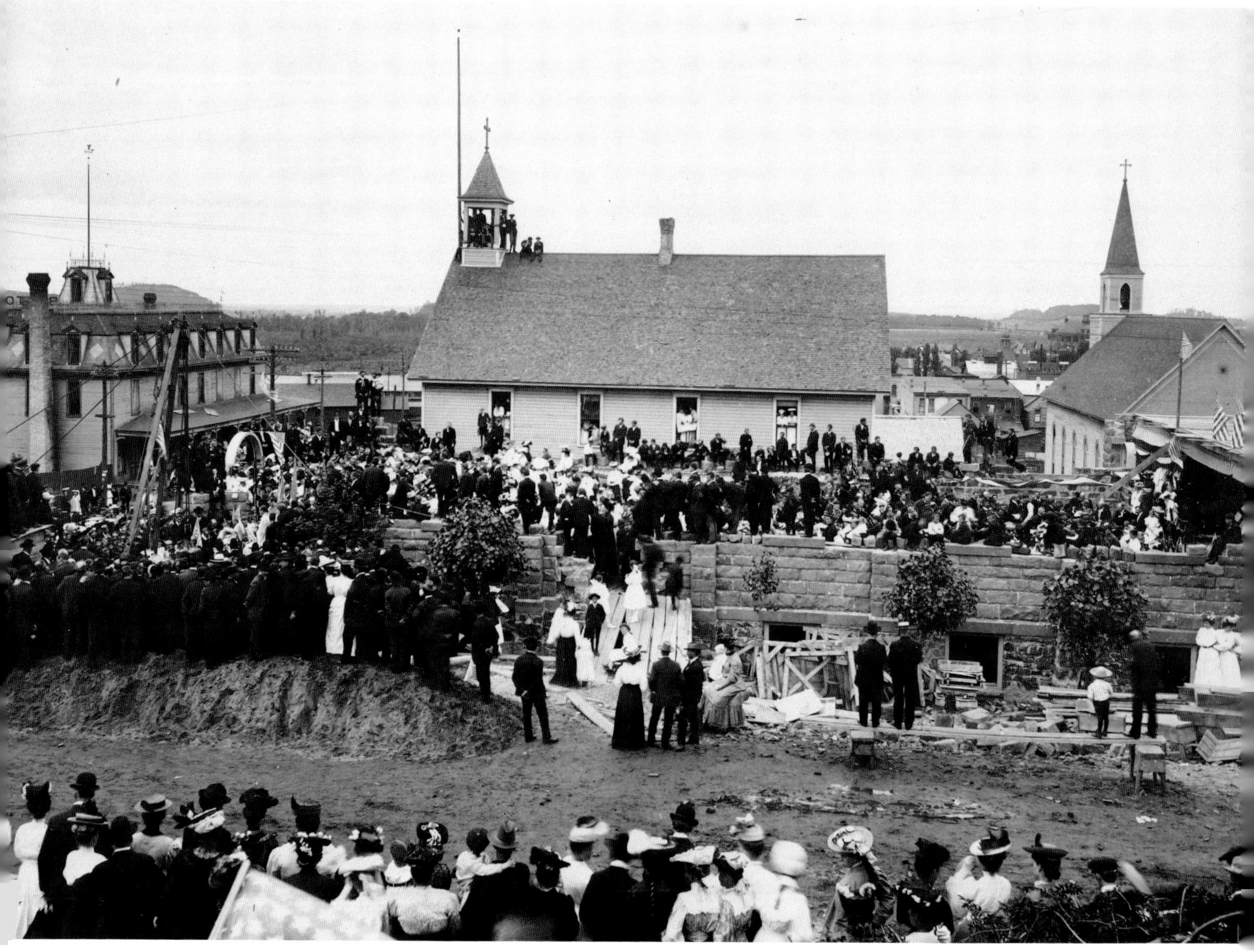

Faiths Diverse

The religious life of Iron county reflected the ethnic diversity of its settlers. Itinerant pastors and priests of various denominations traveled by foot, wagon, or rail to bring the "Good News" to the settlers. Religious services were often held in a settler's home, the town hall, or a school. Within a year or two of being visited by a minister, a congregation usually organized to form a permanent church.

The need for established churches must have been apparent to the faithful who lived in the bawdy mining town of Hurley. Reverend Father Chrysostom Verwyst, who arrived in Bayfield in 1878 to minister to the Ojibwe, was instructed to add Hurley to his 240-mile circuit. He conducted the first church service in Hurley on November 1, 1885. Less than a year later, his congregation began construction of Hurley's first Catholic church, St. Mary of the Seven Dolors. Under the guidance of Father Gilbert Nuono in 1891, Iron county's only Catholic school opened with 120 students staffed by three Franciscan Sisters from Milwaukee. Catholic congregations grew around mining locations in Montreal, Pence, Iron Belt, and the logging town of Saxon. A priest rotated between these mission churches, traveling by rail and, later, by automobile.

Already well-known for indulgence, Hurley also developed a strong religious culture. Presbyterian minister Reverend D.S. Banks visited the Range in 1885 and conducted the first Presbyterian services in February 1886, at Paeske's Hall in Hurley. The lack of a pulpit at Paeske's didn't bother Reverend Banks, who preached in the skating rink. He brought believers from both sides of the river together to form a Union Presbyterian Church with Ironwood. Almost immediately, construction began on a church building. By September 1886, Reverend Banks had a real pulpit to preach from. Another Presbyterian evangelist, Reverend C.L. Harries, knew that men wouldn't attend church in a rough and tumble town like Hurley. He brought the faith to them and set up his pulpit in a pool hall on Silver Street.

Hurley, July 15, 1906. The red sandstone cornerstone of St. Mary's of the Seven Dolors is laid. Officiating at the ceremony was the Papacy's own representative in the United States, the Most Reverend De Medio Falconio. The church was the dream of Father Gilbert Nuono who gathered believers into a functioning congregation and organized support for the creation of a magnificent red sandstone church. The old wooden Catholic Church is the steepled building at right with the Catholic School in the middle. In the distance may be seen the dome-shaped top of Sharey Zedek Synagogue. At left is the Burton House.

First Methodist Episcopal, Mercer

First Presbyterian, Hurley

St. Paul's Lutheran, Hurley

Sharey Zedek Jewish Synagogue, Hurley

Church of the Nazarene, Mercer

Lutheran churches were established along ethnic lines. German settlers organized their church in Hurley in March 1889 under the name "Die Deutsche Evangelische Lutherische St. Paulus Gemeinde U.A.C. in Ironwood und Umgegend." By 1890, St. Paul's had constructed a new church at the corner of Poplar Street and Second Avenue. Finnish Lutheran Churches and Finnish Churches were organized in communities with larger numbers of those Finnish settlers. These ethnic churches helped to keep old country faith and traditions alive.

The railroad played an important role in bringing the faith to Mercer. The first services of the German Evangelical Church were conducted in 1905 by Reverend DeJung who traveled by train from Rhinelander. The first masses at Mercer's new Catholic parish in 1918 were scheduled so that the priest could catch a ride out of town by train or whatever other conveyance was handy.

The Methodists founded churches in Hurley and Mercer. The First Methodist Episcopal Church in Mercer became the first house of worship built in the community in 1908. With gracious Christian hospitality, the Methodists shared their building with the community's German Lutheran and the new Nazarene Church until these congregations built their own places of worship.

Jewish settlers brought their faith to Hurley. The Sharey Zedek congregation organized around 1892. Their first worship services were held in the home of Louis Ladin. In 1895, the congregation built the unique domed synagogue under the direction of Rabbi Rein. At one time, there were over 45 families in the congregation, but with few new immigrants of the faith coming to the community, the Jewish organization faded into history.

Churches not pictured:
Zion Lutheran, Mercer
Northwoods Chapel of Hope, Gurney
New Faith Lutheran, Mercer
St. Isaac Jogues, Mercer
Northwoods Chapel of Hope, Gurney
Our apologies to any congregations that may have been omitted.

St. Anthony's, Pence

Saxon-Gurney Community, Saxon

St. Mary Magdalene, Iron Belt

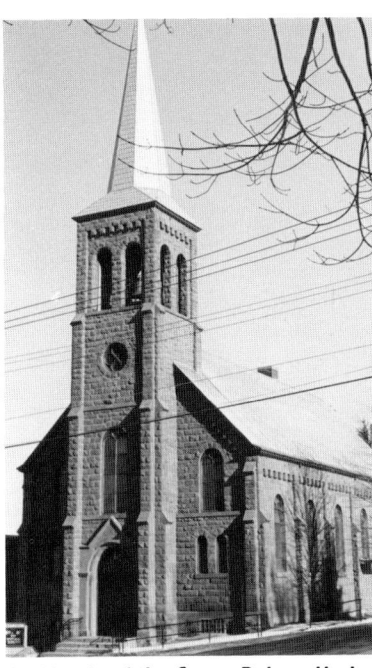

St. Mary's of the Seven Dolors, Hurley

Sacred Heart of Jesus, Montreal

St. Ann's, Saxon

Good Shepherd Lutheran, Missouri Synod, Kimball

Old Faith Lutheran, Mercer

Range Community Bible, Hurley

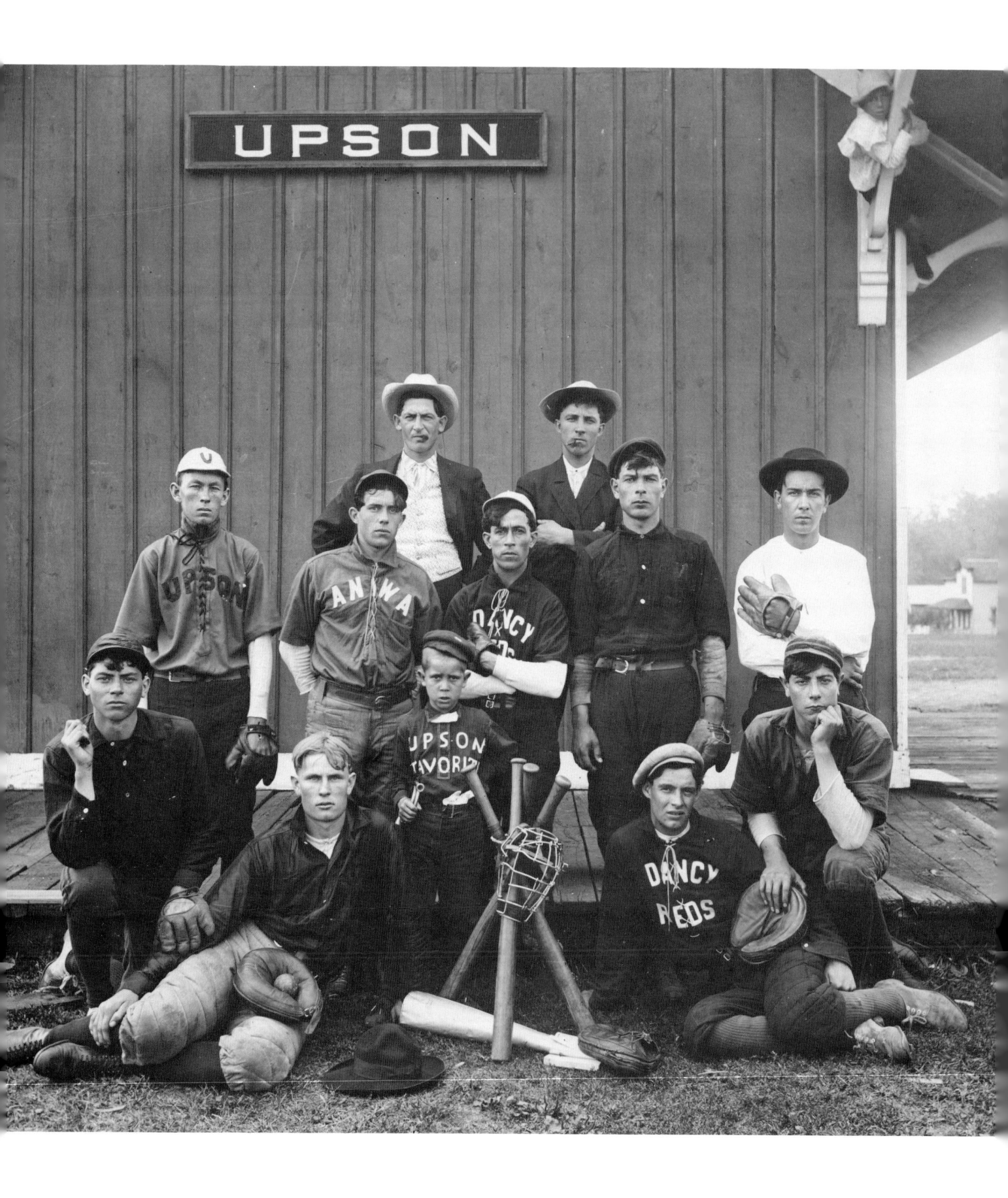
UPSON
UPSON
ANWA
DANCY REDS
UPSON FAVORITE
DANCY REDS

Good Times

It wasn't all work for early settlers. Despite the long hours and back-breaking labor, there was still some leisure time to enjoy pastimes and refresh the spirit.

Settlers had to depend on each other for entertainment. Good times were homemade. When there weren't ball games or parades, people packed picnic lunches and enjoyed leisurely walks to the waterfalls north of Hurley, to Wetzler's Park, Lake Lavina, or Rock Cut Falls. Many people fished and hunted. Some owned summer homes around lakes in Mercer or Springstead and spent their leisure time in the woods. Swimming holes near the Scott and Howe Mill on the Montreal, at Weber Lake, and around Mercer were filled with kids on hot summer days.

Young and old could spend evenings dancing or just enjoying the tunes of the popular local dance bands like the Melodey Orchestra, the J.C. Flanagan Group, the Florian Erspamer band, or Dan's Dance Band. Bonino's Hall was the hot spot on the Range for dancing.

Theaters brought talent from outside the community. Troupes of actors and actresses played the northern Wisconsin theater circuit, arriving in Hurley by train for their performances. The Temple Theater booked big-name drama and vaudeville acts. When moving pictures replaced live stage acts, the Temple was converted to show the silent movies. In Mercer, Mrs. Evenson played the piano for silent films shown on the second floor above the Sweet Shop. For 10¢, children and adults thrilled to the daring adventures of Hoot Gibson and the "Riddle Rider." In the summer, films would sometimes be shown against the white wall of a building in downtown Mercer. The performances delighted residents and amused passengers on passing trains.

Some theaters offered culture of a different sort. Showhouses, like the Central Garden and Ernia Theaters, promoted girl troupes, up to 25 members strong, that sang, danced, and served beer and liquor to patrons. Gambling was often part of the entertainment. The Alcazar Theater had a combined approach. To attract customers to

Upson, c. 1913-1914. The Upson baseball team poses in front of the depot. (l-r, front row) ____ Grew, unidentified, Sneed boy, Hanford Dicky, ____ Grew, (l-r, middle row) Albert Anderson, Walt Hiener, ____ Moss, Grew Lucia, Erb. Lucia, (l-r, back row) Joe Leichtnam, Vincent Flateau. Baseball was very popular in the early 1900s and communities had teams to compete in "friendly" tournament play.

Ironwood, c. 1894. The Hurley Cornet Band meets the Ironwood World's Fair Band. Bands were very popular in the early 1900s. It was as much of a social event for players to come together to practice and perform as it was for an audience to listen. This photo was taken in the front yard of the present Luther L. Wright High School looking east toward Jessieville. Installing wooden sidewalks was a marketing strategy used by real estate agents. They bolstered the confidence of city lot purchasers by giving the community the look of progress, even though it had just been carved out of the stump-infested Cutover.

his acts, owner Charles LeClaire paraded a band up and down Silver Street daily. Once inside, theater-goers could enjoy the show while sipping cold beer served by young hostesses. Many local musicians honed their talents and stage presence while playing backup to showhouse acts.

There were plenty of activities to make the long winter months pass by quickly. Besides opportunities to belong to the many fraternal and social clubs within the county, residents enjoyed skiing, skating, ice fishing, and sledding. The Northland Club was organized under the leadership of E.S. Hagen in 1928 to beat the winter doldrums. Northland volunteers erected a 1,050-foot toboggan slide at their clubhouse at Lake Lavina that propelled sleds as fast as 90 MPH down its iced double track. Winter carnivals, January parades through Hurley, speed skating and motorcycle or auto driving exhibitions on ice may have seemed crazy in the sub-zero temperatures, but they coaxed people out of their warm homes to enjoy the action and each other's company.

▲ Hurley, 1928. The Hurley American Legion Band -Edward L. Cossette Post 58 and members of the American Legion Auxiliary at the dedication of the American Legion building in Hurley. The American Legion Post was organized shortly after the Iron County World War I Homecoming. It was named after Edward L. Cossette of Pence, the first Iron county resident to lose his life in the war. The Auxiliary's mission was to serve "side by side with the men of the Legion in a spirit of unselfish devotion to the well being of the American republic." The Legion provided support for returning veterans and conducted social and patriotic events.

▶ Iron Belt, 1943. The Iron Belt High School Band.

▼ Hurley, c. 1959. The Iron County V.F.W. Junior Drum and Bugle Corps–junior state champions in 1959.

c. 1907. A joint function of the Garibaldi Society of Pence and the Providente Society of Iron Belt. (l-r, front row) Peter Bioletto, Victor Cardini, Ben Endrizzi, Tony Endrizzi, Frank Zandi, Victor Zandi, unidentified, Mike Brentari, Joe Prezzetti, Dominic Cardini, Louis Morgando, Joe Brighenti, Bat Chiolino, Dan Catalino, Albert Magni (?), unidentified boy, Louis Marzari, Sam Trenti, (l-r, second row) Battista Baravetti, Tony Reinerio, unidentified, unidentified, John Tonioni (primo), John Tonioni (secundo), Paradiso Trombi, Pete Brackett, Batista Reinerio, Tony Bertolino, Joe Calvi, Clement Bertagnoli, Anton Urli, Angelo Ferranti, Bernard Testolino, Tony Caligaro, _____ Vernetti, unidentified, (l-r, third row) John Barbalosi, Jim Alfonsi, Bartolomeo Reinerio, Tony Macolati, John Longo-Vigo Rigo, Pete Crevetti, Cominic Peruzzo, Phil Alfonsi, Anton Chiapusio, Guglielmo Cardini, Batista Calvi, John B. Chiapusio, Tony Chiapusio, Frank Giacomello, unidentified, unidentified, Tony Perero, Dan Stomponi, Nicolas Marolla, unidentified, unidentified, Tadio Marolla, (l-r, fourth row) Frank Leone Mancio, Dominic Negri, unidentified, Giaco Calvi, _____ Parero, Rico Baima, unidentified, Silvio Tonioni, Sam Giovanoni, unidentified, Matt Giovanoni, Vincent Calvi, five unidentified members, Dominic Balzan (?), (l-r, fifth row) unidentified, Steve Grevetti (holding flag), eight unidentified members, John Perotti, John Chiapusio, unidentified, unidentified, William Bertagnoli, unidentified, unidentified, Leo Preuss, four unidentified members, Pete Marchetti (head next to flag).

Hurley, c. 1900. Bonino's Hall, on the corner of 1st Avenue and Silver Street, was a favorite meeting place to hold club meetings and dances.

▲ Hurley, c. 1900. The Order of the Owls - Hurley Nest met every second Tuesday at Bonino's Hall. (l-r seated) John Lunney, William Paynter, Judge Peter H. Aspinwall, Sam Hoskins, (l-r, standing) ____ Miller, Patrick Lanzer, John Hennigan, Dr. Dexter Smith, unidentified, Ed Podvin. Order of the Owl members hailed from all walks of life and included a town clerk, judge, powder monkey, saloonkeeper, and physician. Undoubtedly, they functioned as a fraternal club, although their purpose is unknown. Clubs organized for religious, social, and fraternal purposes. By 1912, there were as many as 21 "secret" fraternal societies meeting in Hurley, including the Austrian Tyrol, Bersaglieri di Savia, Catholic Foresters, Odd Fellows, Maccabees, Polish Line of America, and the Scandinavian Help Fellowship.

▶ Hurley, 1938. Leaders of women's groups meet with State Home Extension Leader Miss Blanche Lee to promote home economics work through the leader training method. Women's groups organized in Saxon, Oma, Upson, Gurney, and Iron Belt for a variety of purposes. Most were organized to encourage free discussion of public questions and to mobilize women for social action. Women's clubs promoted social good by purchasing iodine tablets for school children, buying school bells, or sewing bandages for the war effort. Sometimes the emphasis of the clubs extended beyond the social realm. The first county advertising brochure was sponsored by the County Federation of Women's Clubs in 1938.

▶ June, 1989 - Kimball. Members of the National Finnish American Festival keep the traditions alive as they celebrate "Juhanus," the mid-summer festival. The organization was formed after the close of the mines in 1964 "...to further the economic development of the area and to promote and perpetuate the aspects of the Finnish culture."

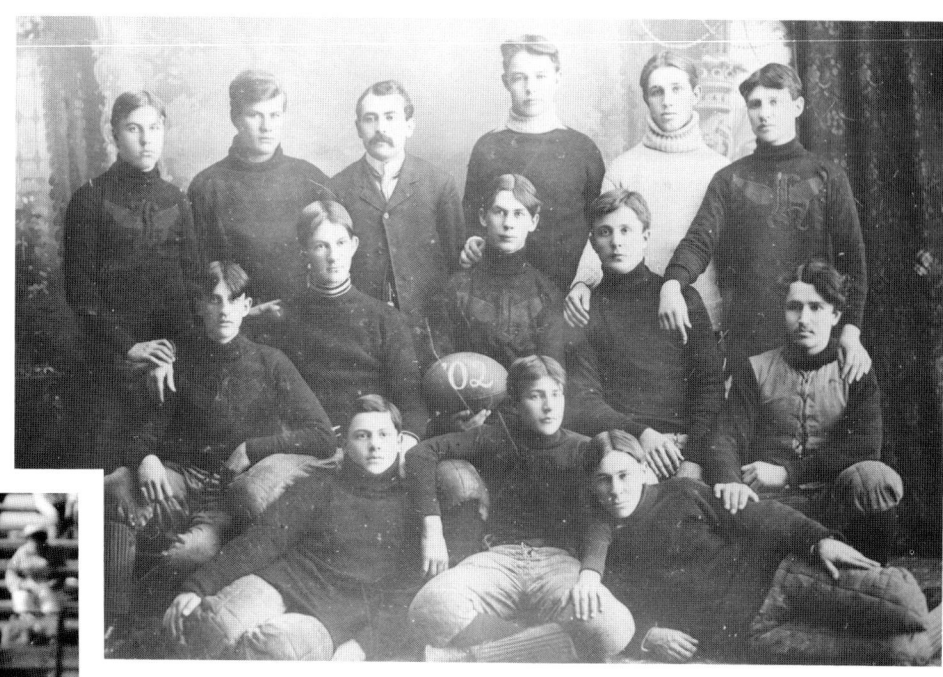

Hurley, 1902. The Hurley High School football team. (l-r, front row) Fred Galardi, Joe Charbonneau, Martin Vickers, (l-r, middle row) Delore Charbonneau, Bud Shean, John Taylor, ____ Grimm, Pete Bonino, (l-r, back row) R. Sackett, Danny Smith, the coach, Buck Nelson, Leo Breighton, Bidow Charbonneau. (Inset) Hurley, 1992. Hurley "Midget" football, Hurley versus Three Lakes. "... They call us Midgets as we are known, We're full of pep and rarin' to go. So fight, fight, fight with all your might; and we'll celebrate tonight,"–Hurley School Song.

Hurley, 1949. WIAA State Basketball Champions - the Hurley High School Basketball Team. (l-r, front) Noel Mattei, Carl Hermanson, Pete Savant, Wayland Baron, Len Bartolutti, (l-r, back) William Anonich, Jim Tocci, Bob Rainaldo, Eugene Martino, Coach Carl Vergamini (not shown: Clayton Corrigan). Despite a bitter cold March night, over 10,000 people turned out to welcome home the Hurley Midgets State Basketball Champs after beating LaCrosse Logan in a 37-36 heartstopper. Their Greyhound bus was greeted at the county line by supportive fans from Mercer. A caravan of 300 cars followed them into Hurley where a parade and community banquet welcomed them. The city fire siren blew so long in their honor that it wore out and–at the end--could only burp static.

▶ Hurley, 1924. The Hurley High School Girls Basketball Team. (l-r, front) Virginia Varalli, Ethel Charnes, Captain Laura Douville, Clara Gutowski, Nellie Ziff, (l-r, back) Coach Margaret Chiono, Esther Endrizzi, Jane Hambley, Helen Frigo, Jennie Morris. The Hurley girls played teams from as far away as Ewen, Mich. In the 1930s, girls basketball disappeared as a team sport and did not return until the 1980's when state law required that sports opportunities once again be provided to girls as well as boys.

▲ Mercer, 1916. Another girls' sports team, the 1916 Mercer Girls Basketball Tigerettes. (l-r) Nellie Steiner, Madeline Theriault, Grace Thompson, unidentified, unidentified. "...Cling to our Mercer High, may our memories never die. Loyal fans we will be till eternity. Hail to thee our Mercer High," –Mercer School Song

▲ Mercer, 1916. (l-r, front) Gaylord Thompson, Herb Peter, (l-r, back) Vern Hodson, George Harper, Alfred Lee. With only five members on the team, the 1916 Mercer Tiger cagers must have been as tough as the girls.

◀ Mercer, 1992. Mercer High School celebrates winning the State WIAA Girls Volleyball Championship. (l-r) Shawn Thompson, Mike Gentile, School Administrator Jack English.

93

▲ Hurley, c. 1910. Hurley's Italian heritage gave rise to ethnic celebrations that are still commemorated today during Hurley's "Italian Days."

◄ Hurley, c. 1970. A banner welcomes "Paisanos" to what was then called the "Dago Days" festival on Silver Street.

▼ Hurley, 1958. The Memorial Day parade in Hurley progresses from Silver Street to the Memorial Building. Parades were a popular pastime and a real community event, whether they were for fun or a more somber commemoration.

▲ Upson, c. 1987. The Paavo Nurmi Marathon has been run from Upson to Hurley each August for the past 24 years. The 26-mile, 385-yard course winds through the Penokee foothills and old mining communities along Highway 77 before reaching the finish line on Silver Street. The race was named after Paavo Nurmi, "the Flying Finn," who was called the greatest distance runner of all time. It is considered one of the toughest marathons in the country.

▶ Montreal, 1992. The "Battling Bruisers," representing the Hurley Police Department and the Iron County Sheriff's Department, prepare to square off against the Ironwood Police Department's "Boys in Blue" team in a charity baseball game. (l-r) Wisconsin Governor Tommy Thompson, Hurley Detective Sergeant Ken Colassaco, Sheriff Richard Ekmark, Hurley Police Chief Ted Erspamer, District Attorney Jodie Bednar, and "Suds" Morichetti. The friendly grudge match between the two teams raises money for Iron County's Law Enforcement Youth Fund.

▶ Mercer, 1950. All community organizations and citizens are invited to celebrate in Mercer's 4th of July Parade.

▲ Mercer, 1940. The Mother-Daughter Banquet was an annual social event that the community looked forward to. It was a special time together to help renew bonds between women of all ages who might be separated by distance, family commitments, or work during the year. Mercer residents recognized the need for a building where community events like this could be held. They organized a WPA project in 1936 to create a unique log community building. Finnish craftsmen used 80-foot Norway pine logs, joining them with only ax and auger. No nails, chinking, or power tools were used. Logs were hoisted into place by hand, and heavy wooden handmade pins were driven into the logs at four-foot intervals.

◄ Mercer, 1988. An unidentified contestant tries his skill at "loon calling" for Loon Days' Master of Ceremonies, Debbie Brandt. Loon Days has been held on the first Wednesday in August since 1980. The event brings about 10,000 visitors to Mercer, the "Loon Capital of the World."

(Upper Right) Saxon, 1938. Produce, conservation displays, and 4-H demonstrations were jam-packed into the exhibit room of the Saxon School and Community Fair. Fairs gave rural youth the chance to exhibit the skills they had learned through 4-H and school. The first fair was held in 1923 at Saxon because it was the only community interested in the event. Exhibits were displayed in the Saxon School. An exhibitor could win a blue ribbon and a premium award as high as 75¢ for a winning peck of potatoes. There was no state aid for fairs in those days. Ribbon-winning pies, cakes, and canned goods had to be auctioned off to make money to run the fair. In 1938, the Saxon School Fair Association reorganized under the name "Iron County Fair Association" and went county-wide.

(Above) Saxon. c. 1970. Exhibitors show off their prize cattle for a judge at the Iron County Fair. Livestock are traditionally the most popular exhibits. The sign on the old cattle barn promotes the fairgrounds as being "in the heart of Iron county dairy industry."

(Right) Saxon, 1992. Motorized events like ATV racing are a crowd-pleasing addition to the traditional events offered at the Iron County Fair. "The community fair awakens community pride, spirit, and life. It includes every person in the neighborhood and every organization in it. It is a day on which the whole countryside plays and renews acquaintances..."–1923 Iron County Fair Premium Book

▲ Park Falls, c. 1906. "Blueberry Special" trains would occasionally be run by the Roddis Lumber Company on Sundays to take Park Falls residents on berry-picking excursions in Iron county. Dressed in their Sunday finery, the pickers found seats on bales of hay and enjoyed the impromptu "flat car" party while riding the rails to the choicest berry patches.

◄ Kimball, 1913. The steep incline of Eagle Bluff made a perfect landing for a ski jump, although this jumper looks somewhat out of control. Even those who didn't ski could enjoy a diversion from the long winter by watching the action.

◄ Saxon, 1927. This fine catch of fish will soon become the family's dinner. (l-r), Martin Niemi, Werner Niemi, Harold Niemi. Iron county's first recorded "fish story" was told by William F. Turner in 1874. As he recounted in his diary: "There we were, 80 miles from the nearest white settlement without a mouthful to eat. Arriving at the Manitowish River that night, I tore off a few strips from the white shirt Briggs wore for a fish line, fastened the hook on it, caught a frog, and threw it in for a fish. As soon as the hook struck the water, a big black bass took it and away he went with our only fish hook and a part of poor Briggs' shirttail in his mouth."

Mercer, 1928. Mercer had a nine-hole, 2,361-yard golf course with tennis facilities and croquet on the lawn. Green fees were only $1.00. Construction began in 1961 on the 18-hole Eagle Bluff Golf Course in Kimball, which is now the county's only course. Golfing has become a popular summer sport with local residents, and the scenic beauty and challenge of Eagle Bluff lures many visiting golfers to its fairways.

Saxon, c. 1990. Saxon Harbor offers Lake Superior access to recreational boaters, deep-sea charter fishing trips, and agate-seeking beachcombers. The picturesque harbor and adjoining park have been operated by Iron county since it was designated a county park site in 1922.

Iron Belt, c. 1968. Whitecap Ski Area was one of the first downhill ski areas to open in Big Snow Country. Its location on the Penokee Range gives it the highest vertical drop and longest runs of any area hill and guarantees consistent snowfall. While local settlers skied on barrel staves, downhill skiing is now a multi-million dollar industry in Iron county. Whitecap has expanded to accommodate the growing downhill ski trade, adding chairlifts, snowmaking, and deluxe lodging.

Hurley, 1992. Snowmobilers leave the Hurley Holiday Inn for a day on Iron county's 400-mile system of groomed snowmobile trails. Snowmobiling has come a long way from the days of the first oil-belchers that were lucky to go a few miles without a breakdown. Volunteer groups, like the White Thunder Riders and Mercer Sno-A-Goers, create highways of groomed trails that connect lodges, taverns, and entertainment spots. Snowmobiling has grown to be a significant winter tourism industry. Winter is no longer the "off season" for many county businesses.

Pence, 1991. Members of the Penokee Rangers Nordic Ski Club prepare to track-set cross country ski trails. (l-r, kneeling) Frank "Kluchie" Maffesanti, Charlie Zinsmaster, (on snowmobile) Jim Butterbrodt. Cross country skiing is a growing "silent sport." Volunteer clubs, like the Penokee Rangers and Mecca Ski Club of Mercer, groom and maintain trails that are enjoyed by local residents and visitors.

"The time is long overdue for the decent people of Hurley to get together and demand that the last remnants of vice and indecency be chased out of our city. We are trying to get industry. No business is going to come to Hurley when we get yellow journalism...by allowing what is down the street to give us a bad name. Decent people can no longer ignore the lower block. City officials can no longer look at it as a necessary economic evil." *–Iron County Miner,* Nov. 27, 1964.

▸ Hurley, c. 1960. Hurley's lower block in its heyday added a spicy touch to Hurley's history and gave it the reputation of being "The Life of the Northwoods."

(Above) Hurley, c. 1950. The Club Carnival was one of many of Hurley's bars that promised fun galore for its patrons. The city's reputation for gambling, girls, and good times has brought fun-seekers to Hurley since the 1880's.

(Center Right) Hurley, c. 1971. Crackdowns on vice, gambling, and prostitution signaled the decline of the lower block. In 1971, several lower-block establishments burned down, including the Club Carnival.

(Right) Hurley, 1991. (l-r) Pam Bresnahan, Robert Bresnahan, Chef Walter Backlund. Hurley's sparkling nightlife and fine dining still appeal to those seeking a good time out on the town.

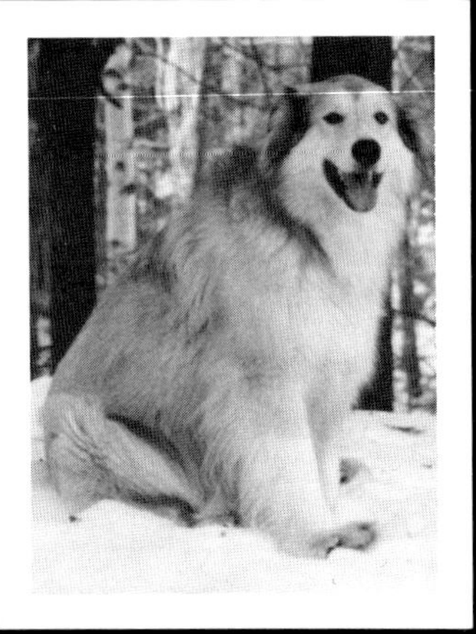

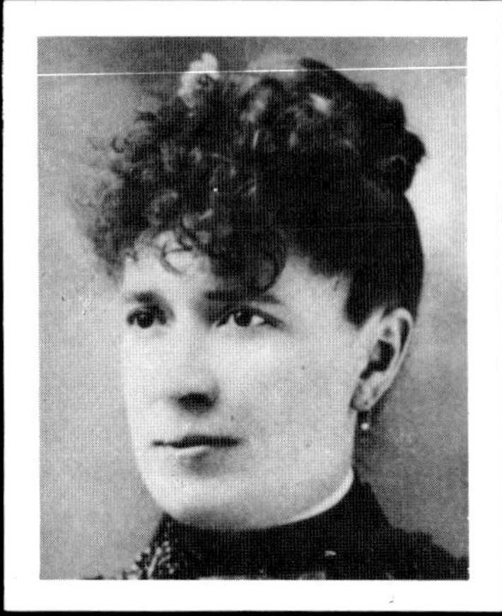

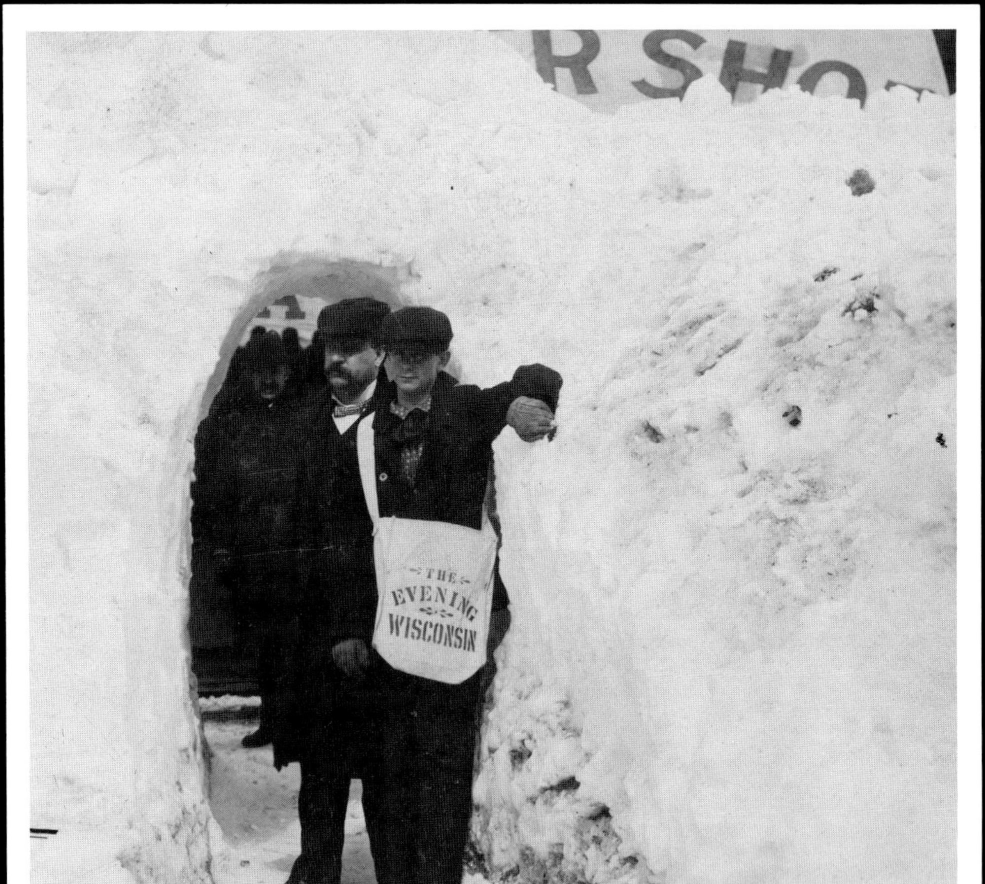
R SHO
THE
EVENING
WISCONSIN

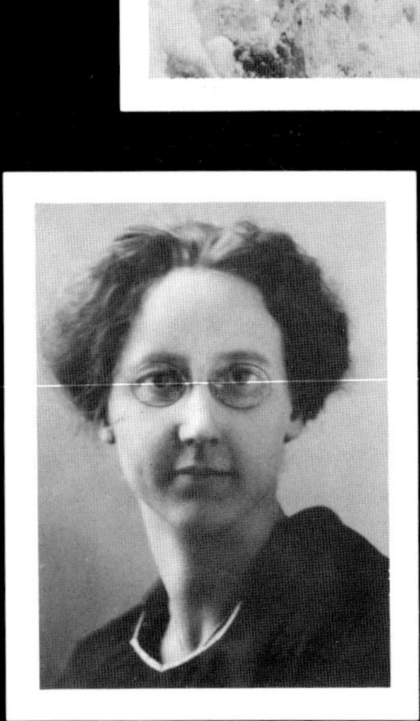

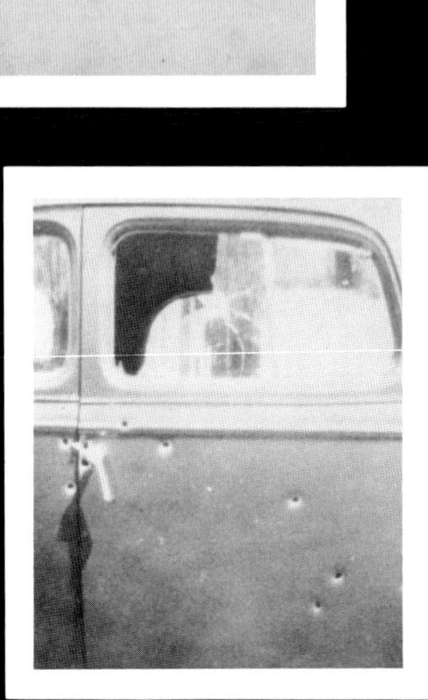

Iron County Centennial News

Hurley's Talking Dog Convicts Man!

Hurley, 1890. Henry Tarrish's brilliant collie dog, Shep, testified today as the key witness of the murder of his owner. Tarrish, a crippled logger, and his constant companion, Shep, had disappeared from town over eight years ago. Hunters found a body, identified as that of Tarrish, with two bullet holes in his head this November. There was no sign of Shep. Private detective Lewis A. Potter broke the case when he found Shep performing as a dancing dog in a traveling medicine show in Antigo. Potter traced the dog back to an Indian trapper named "Horseface" who, upon seeing the dog, confessed to being involved in Tarrish's murder along with an ex-convict named Peter Korn. At the trial, Korn denied ever seeing Tarrish or the dog. When Shep took the witness stand, he growled and snapped at Korn. Upon Shep's eloquent testimony, Korn was sentenced to life imprisonment at Waupun. He is the only criminal known to have been convicted by the "spoken" testimony of a dog. (Upper Left)

Good news or bad, newspaper headlines announced the tragedies and triumphs of life in Iron county. The stories on this page accompany the photos on the preceding page.

Extra! Extra!

Snowstorm Buries Hurley's Main Street!

Hurley, 1899. Businesses in Hurley were forced to tunnel out to the street to allow passage of commerce and customers after snow and high winds buried the Range. Judge Griff Thomas (with moustache) surveys the results of the storm that left the community paralyzed. (Center)

Lovely Ghost Haunts Mercer Cemetery!

Mercer, c. 1980. Several reliable witnesses report seeing the apparition of Eleda Benson in the Mercer cemetery. The young woman came to Mercer by train each Memorial Day during the 1940s and 1950s to put flowers on her parents' graves. The ghost has been seen several times lately and appears dressed in pink during the summer and black in the winter months.
(Lower Left)

Happy 100!

Car Riddled With 17 Bullet Holes As Feds Mistake Local Men for Gangsters!

Manitowish Waters, April 22, 1934. Federal agents with itchy trigger fingers mistakenly opened fire on a car belonging to Mellen CCC camp worker Eugene Boisoneau. They believed it was being driven by John Dillinger, America's Public Enemy #1. Boisoneau was killed instantly, and passengers John Hoffman of Mercer and John Morris were wounded. According to Morris, the men had gone to Little Bohemia Lodge for a few beers and never intended to get caught in the middle of an FBI stakeout. At the sound of the first shots, the real gang split up and escaped from the unguarded lakeshore side of the resort. Federal agent W. Carter Baum was killed and Spider Lake Constable Carl Christensen critically wounded in a car chase that followed.
(Lower Right)

Lotta Morgan Murdered!

Hurley, April 10, 1890. The body of Lotta Morgan, Hurley variety actress and lady of the evening, was found near Crocker's woodshed. She had been struck in the head with an ax. The murder weapon was found nearby. Police also found an unfired revolver at her feet. Theft is not suspected as the motive since Morgan's diamond earrings and rings were not taken. Police have arrested Terry Day (alias Terry Riley) after they found a bloody coat in his possession. There is rumor that the murder may have been part of plot involving Hurley's power structure. A funeral will be held at the Opera Hall. A large turnout is expected. Miss Morgan was considered "one of the prettiest women on the Range". She would have turned 29 in three days.
(Upper Right)

G. A. ALEXANDER,
Justice of the Peace.
CONVEYANCING and COLLECTIONS
Promptly attended to.
AGENT U. S. EXPRESS CO.
Offices on Silver Street.

Keep Off The Grass! Hurley, 1923. The snowstorm of '23 may have been a lot of fun to Hurley children, but it isolated the community from the rest of the world for three days. The blizzard brought heavy snow and extreme cold of 20-30 degrees below zero, freezing many water pipes. A second, more powerful snowstorm buried Hurley in drifts as high as 15-20 feet in January 1938. The two-day storm was whipped by hurricane-force winds from the north. Snow removal equipment, normally effective in the worst storms, could not open roads. Hurley was stranded and running low on supplies, such as milk, by the time the first trains were able to arrive two days later.

Hurley, October 30, 1952. A blistering hot fire, thought to have been started by the burning of grass, destroyed five lumber sheds at the Erspamer Lumber Yard and scorched several homes nearby. Fire was a constant threat to the wooden storefronts of early Hurley. Three great fires, the Gogebic Meat Company and Alcazar Theater fires in 1887 and the Klondike Theater fire in 1901, nearly consumed all of Main Street. Each time, plucky Hurley business people rebuilt. Other large fires visited Hurley in 1912, 1918, and 1937.

▲ Hurley, May 12, 1894. Fire broke out on the fourth floor of the Burton House, but was brought under control quickly by the Hurley Fire Department. The building was billed as fireproof, since every space in the walls and floor was stuffed with non-flammable mineral wool.

▶ Hurley, February 1947. The Burton House, once Hurley's finest hotel, burned to the ground. All that remained of the 100 rooms and stately promenade was a blackened chimney and memories of the booming 1880's. The old hotel had lost it hauteur and was run down over the years by a string of owners. Only 10 transient "jacks" and a family were staying inside at the time. They escaped without injury. All of Silver Street was showered with embers as the "grande dame" of Hurley was swallowed up by the intense fire in little less than an hour.

◄ Mercer, July 14, 1958. A tornado struck downtown Mercer without warning, causing extensive damage downtown. There were no serious injuries. Iron county was declared a disaster area, which helped businesses receive low-cost loans to rebuild.

◄ Gile, 1928. Rapid melting of the winter's record snowfall of 207.9 inches caused severe flooding on the west branch of the Montreal River and washed out the Highway 77 bridge. In the distance, the No. 5 shaft of the Montreal Mine can be seen.

◄ Hurley, July 4, 1992. Forty-three years to the day, the east branch of the Montreal flooded again, as it did on July 4, 1949. Saturated soils could not handle the torrential rains that the Range received during the spring and early summer months. Volunteers sandbagged homes in the "flats," and bridges to Ironwood were closed. Damage was kept to a minimum.

Montreal, c. 1938. Patrons at Noel Mattei's tavern in Montreal enjoy some spirited camaraderie. Hurley's streets were filled with as many as 200 cars on April evenings in 1918 as people loaded up on alcohol in anticipation of wartime prohibition. Prohibition was the product of the moral idealism and the stresses of World War I. Some saloonkeepers took a chance that prohibition would not limit all alcoholic beverages and continued to serve 2 3/4 alcohol content beer.

Hurley had little reason to close its saloons. At $500 a license per year, taverns were a major source of municipal revenue. In June, almost on the eve of the enactment of the Volstead Act, which defined intoxicating liquor as any beverage containing over 1/2 of 1 per cent of alcohol, the city granted six wholesale and 53 retail liquor licenses.

In October, when Uncle Sam made it clear that Hurley would be "bone dry," over 50 "soft drink" parlors opened where saloons had once been. Even beer signs had to be removed. Fifty-five saloon owners and distributors, representing $30,000 in potential license money to Hurley, were officially notified by federal marshals that the bone dry law would be enforced to the letter.

Newspapers lamented, "good-bye kicking ginger ale," but enterprising Hurley saloonkeepers had as much as a traincar load of beer secretly stored at each of their premises. Violations of prohibition continued. In December 1920, Deputy U.S. Marshal William Pugh led a raid on Silver Street that netted 57 saloonkeepers and bartenders in violations of the Prohibition Act. The case was dismissed in 1923 due to insufficient evidence and illegal search warrants.

Hurley wasn't about to let Prohibition limit its lively downtown trade. Bootleg liquor and home brew flowed into and out of the area. In October 1921, federal marshals were tipped off that a booze caravan was enroute from Milwaukee to Hurley. The procession was stopped in Minocqua, and the situation turned ugly. In the shootout that followed, one Hurley man was killed.

Federal marshals, masquerading as lumberjacks, found that after five years of strict enforcement of prohibition, they were still able to find an ample supply of moonshine in Hurley. The country's experiment in prohibition failed, but it only added to the legend and mystique of Hurley.

▲ Mercer, 1916. Charlie Comiskey, owner of the Chicago White Sox baseball team, built this log lodge on Trude Lake as a place where he and his ballplayers could relax and unwind after a hectic season. Comiskey and Ban Johnson, Commissioner of the American league, named the camp the "Jerome Fishing and Hunting Club." The surrounding area was enclosed with a 16-foot tall fence. Inside, Comiskey kept elk, buffalo, deer, and a tame moose named Bill. The camp was the site of many hunting and fishing parties. A special cabin was built for Comiskey, named the "Home Plate." The home base plate from the 1906 World Series hung over the door.

◄ Saxon, October 1961. Saxon residents got the opportunity to "star" as extras in the production, "Adventures of a Young Man," that was filmed on location in Saxon and Mellen. Roberta Steuers, Gail Holm Rowe, Leone Damgard, Beatrice Lahti, Betty Bluse, Marilyn Baribeau, Irene Smith, Martha Smith, Joyce Bluse Don LaFortune, Marvin Innes, John Chiapusio, Walter Damgard, Gene Norman, George Baker, Con Peterson, and Charlie Steele were among those on screen. Saxon was transformed by Hollywood magic to resemble a small Upper Peninsula town in 1916 for the film based on the boyhood of Ernest Hemingway.

Famous People Who Visited Iron County

Benjamin Harrison, the 23rd President of the United States and a Republican, is listed in the Burton House Register as a guest during the 1888 election campaign. A dinner was served in the main dining room in his honor and he gave a short speech at the railway station before deparrting.

Grover Cleveland, the Democrat who served as President both before and after Benjamin Harrison, also stayed at the Burton House. He arrived near the end of his second term in 1894. Instead of campaigning for office, Cleveland was on a tour of industrial centers to quiet unrest associated with the Pullman railroad workers strike in Chicago.

Sarah Bernhardt, the actress celebrated as the finest of her era, made at least three appearances in Hurley between 1903 and 1910. She played at several of Hurley's opera houses and theatres.

Edwin Booth was the distinguished actor and brother of the infamous assassin of Abraham Lincoln, John Wilkes Booth. Shortly before his death at age 59, Edwin Booth appeared in a play at the Alcazar Theatre in Hurley.

Gilda Gray, the "Shimmy Shimmy Girl" of the silent movie era, passed through Hurley several times early in her career. She returned in later years to see her son, Marty, who lived in Hurley, perform in local theaters.

Over the years, hundreds of entertainers passed through Hurley's night spots on their way up and down the career ladder. Among those recorded as having performed on Silver Street are Harry James, Johnny Paycheck, John Conlee, Tommy Cash, the Grass Roots and the Coasters.

The Colgate family were pioneer residents of Hurley. They built a huge mansion in Hurley, but left after only a few years. They moved to Chicago so they could keep a closer tab on the toothpaste industry.

Edna Ferber stayed in Iron and Gogebic counties while gathering material for her book, *Come and Get It*. While investigating the lives of lumbermen and tavernkeepers she encountered anti-Semitic treatment. Ferber finished the first draft of her book at Lake Gogebic and avoided the Hurley area.

John F. Kennedy, campaigning in what was then the crucial Wisconsin presidential primary election of 1960, visited Iron county along with several members of his family. He gave a campaign speech on the corner of 2nd and Silver.

Hubert H. Humphrey was Kennedy's most serious rival in the 1960 Wisconsin primary. He also campaigned in Iron county, along with his son, Skip, who, in 1993, is the Attorney General of Minnesota.

Hurley, 1960. John F. Kennedy working for votes on Silver Street.

▲ Iron Belt, 1919. This temporary monument was set up for the Iron Belt World War I homecoming to honor the local boys who would not return home. Five of the 11 Iron county soldiers who lost their lives in World War I died overseas of pneumonia.

▼ Iron Belt, 1919. (l-r) Emil Hardy, Teda Carjala, Syma Lypi, Bill Carjola Both men and women supported the military effort during World War I. Women served as nurses, sewed bandages, and made do with rationed foodstuffs. A large homecoming for all Iron county vets was held in Hurley and featured a band concert, street dance, and evening dance at Bonino's Hall. This was the war to end all wars. Never again would Iron county sons or daughters need to be called away from home to fight.

▼ Hurley, c. 1941. Draftees from Iron county await transport by rail to military induction camps. The attack on Pearl Harbor on December 7, 1941 abruptly changed America's undecided position in the world's struggles against the Axis powers. World War II had come to Iron county, for those who went to fight and for those who waited behind for them to return.

Iron County's Most Honored Who Died in the Service of Their Country

World War I	World War II		Korean War	Vietnam War
Eric Aho	Uno Annala	Eli Kovacevich	Charles Baron, Jr.	No known war dead
Robert Arbelius	Angelo Bottacin	Ernest Lahti	Stanley Conhartoski	
Herman Blise	Joseph Darin	Paul Orsonne	Charles Di Ulio	
Edward Cossette	Frederick Durand	Raymond Palmquist	Stanley Kountney	
Adam Demaraski	Gerald Effenger	Tarino Pelto	Jerome Misuraco	
John Grenda	Frank Ehler	Leo Penrose	Adolph Snarski	
Orrin Poole	Lawrence Fassino	Angelo Prarizzi	Leonard Sullivan	
Franklin Hawley	Marvin Gamache	Arthur Ritchie		
Fred Richards	Harry Green	Bartley Roberts		
Thomas Trione	Arthur Hariu	Allan Saarnio		
William Weber	Donald Harries	Bernhardt Semberg		
Antoine Zuchowski	John Hovanec	Carl Swanson		
	Willard Johnson	John Swearingen		
	Peter Kacala	Holger Thompson		
	Robert Karpinski	Harry Turgasen		
	Hugo Kivisto	Edwin White		
	Eli Koski	Walter Zuchowski		

These lists have been compiled from official United States Department of Defense rolls, supplied by the Iron County Veterans Service Office. Neither state nor federal veterans departments claim that these lists are complete. We apologize if we have missed the name of any man or woman who died in service. We salute all of these men and all veterans for their sacrifices and contributions to our country.

Mercer, c. 1960. Memorial Day.

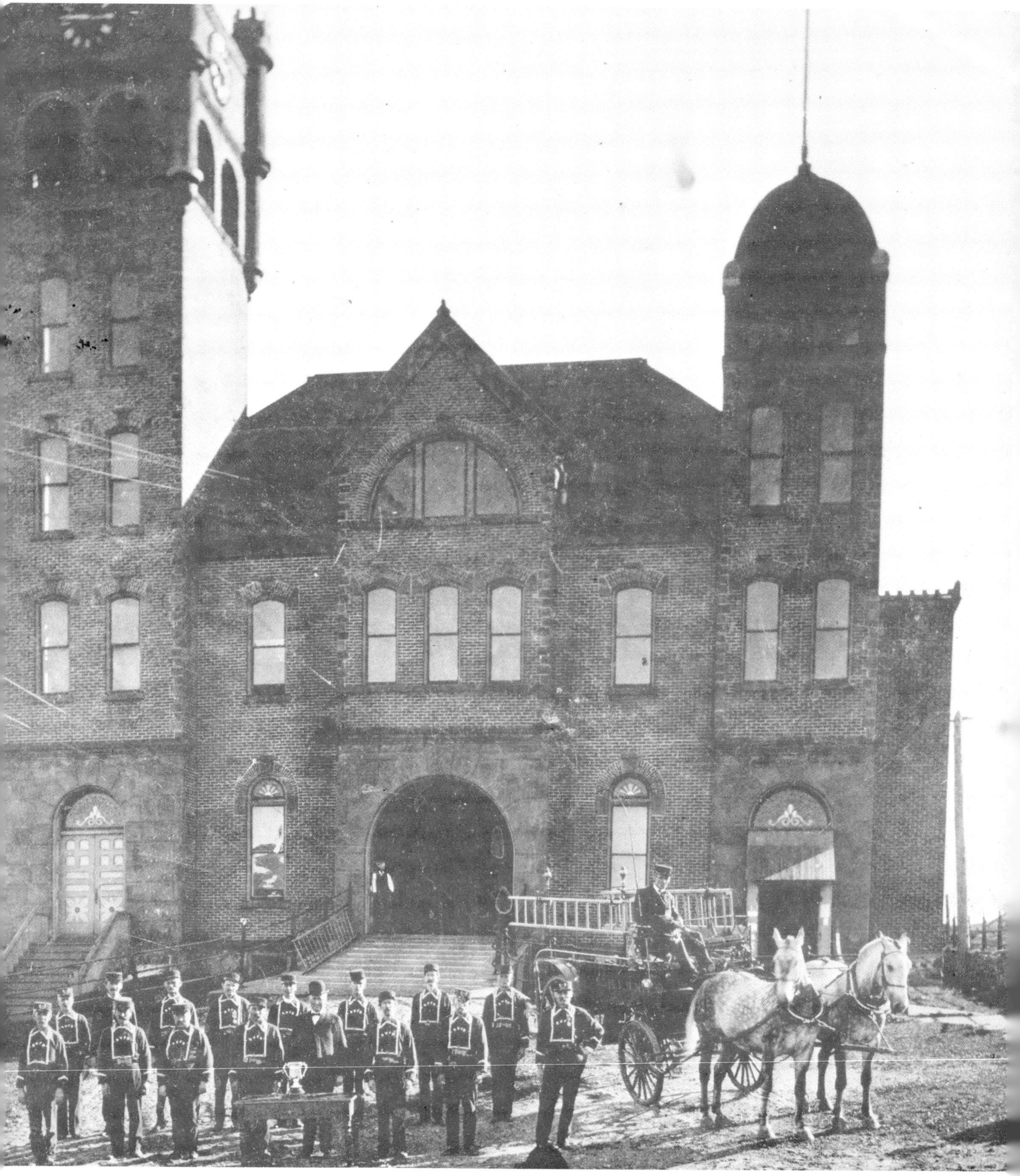

Government in the County

"A county seat is of no particular importance to a town. We have no doubt that the generous people of Ashland would be very willing to divide the honor with Hurley. Honor is all our people are after, anyway. We have all the wealth we need" -*Gogebic Iron Tribune,* February 5, 1887.

The area we know now as Iron county has been shuffled between the boundaries of many older Wisconsin counties. In 1836, it was part of a large Crawford County that included all Wisconsin lands west of the Wisconsin River. In 1840, portions were included in St. Croix County. Another division occurred in 1850 which placed it in the new LaPointe and Marathon Counties. It fell within the borders of Ashland and Marathon Counties in 1870. By 1893, it was included within the boundaries of Ashland County and most of it was called the "Town of Vaughn".

Although the move to "secede" from Ashland County began more than a decade before the actual creation of Iron county, the issue really began to heat up in 1887. Many settlers felt that the timberland in the Town of Vaughn had been taxed to build the streets and sidewalks of Ashland. Now the valuable iron mines of Hurley were booming and the community's wealth and population growing. Ashland would have another source of income to drain to replace the fast-disappearing timber tax revenues. If taxation wasn't enough of a sting, the 40-mile trek through dense forest between Hurley and the county seat of Ashland severely limited Hurley's involvement in county government.

The unpalatable combination of taxation without representation prompted 800 irate town residents to sign a petition requesting that a new county be created from parts of Ashland County. Hurley would be the seat of the new county, which they proposed would be named "Mills County".

Hurley, c. 1900. The original Iron County Courthouse was built as the hall for the Town of Vaughn in 1893. It was sold to Iron County in 1894 for $32,000. The cost of the clock was extra, which some residents thought was an extravagant use of public funds. Although the state legislature created Iron County, no provision was made to house the new government. The first county board met for several months in a shack, then moved to a room above the old Iron Exchange Bank. John C. Flannagan, first county clerk, recalled, "For quite a while, I had to carry all the important [county] documents around in my pocket."

◀ Hurley, c. 1924. Mrs. Luella Trier was the eighth County Treasurer, serving from 1924-1933.

▼ Carey, c. early 1920's. (l-r) Matt Kinnunen with team, Swan Hanson, Sr. with team, Gust Hemming, Matt Wakliini, Gust Luoma, Salomon Mannikko, Matt Maki, Gust Kolu, Frank Nyman. Volunteers assembled to fill in a low spot on Lampi Road in the Town of Carey. Spring Road Day was an annual affair when residents could work off town taxes by volunteering to work on the roads. They could earn a larger credit if more men from a family came to work or if a worker brought horse teams and wagons. Road maintenance was entirely a responsibility of the towns, and travel conditions between towns varied greatly. In 1912, the state passed legislation to create the county highway departments. As an incentive to do so, the new law gave counties and municipalities the opportunity to receive aid for building highways.

The proposal immediately encountered controversy. The *Ashland Press* was the first to react, accusing Hurley that the secession was engineered by a few ambitious men who wanted political office. The tabloid warned of impending doom from the burden of taxes that the new county would have to assume if separated from Ashland county.

Despite the warnings, a bill creating the County of Mills was drafted, passed the state assembly in March 1887, and was forwarded to the senate. A new county might have been created then if it were not for the actions of Ashland Senator George F. Merrill. Merrill delayed the proposal on two counts: that Hurley's largest taxpayers were against it and that the area simply did not have enough people to organize a county. The bill failed, and the political bad blood between Hurley and Ashland became bitter.

Merrill successfully held Iron County at bay for three more years. In September 1890, he did not run again for office. This time, momentum to create a separate new county would not be stopped. Iron County was created by action of the state legislature on March 3, 1893 from parts of Ashland County and four townships of Oneida County. It was one of the last four of Wisconsin's 72 counties to be created.

▲ Hurley, 1990. The new Iron county courthouse was completed in 1975. Twelve years earlier, in 1963, the county board had selected a portion of Boston Park on Germania Hill as the site to construct a new courthouse to replace the aging building on Iron Street. Estimated costs for the new building were $480,000, but the plan was dropped after the county board received a letter from the Cary Mine union objecting to its construction.

Iron County Officials - Then and Now

	Then	Now		Then	Now
Circuit Judge	John K. Parish	Patrick J. Madden	Sheriff	John F. Sullivan	Richard Ekmark
Court Reporter	Joseph Cover	Nancy Colasacco	Undersheriff	Owen Sullivan	Robert Baldauf
County Judge	Thomas Boden	(position eliminated)	Highway Commissioner	F.B. Goodman	Robert Massoglia
Register in Probate	Viola Fish	Mary DeZur & Linda Kuduk	Director of Relief	Charles A. Noren	Lawrence Samardich
Clerk of Court	Sanford Goodell	Virginia Giacomino	(Dir. Dept. of Human Services)		
		Nadya Kangas, Deputy	County Nurse	Marie Kiernan	Judy Kunath
District Attorney	Patrick G. Lennon	Jodie Bednar	Forestry Dept. Adm.	E.F. Dietz	Tom Salzmann
County Clerk	John C. Flannagan	George G. Reed	UW-Extension		
		Jean M. Grasso, Deputy	Ag/Resource Agent	Dan Shaffer	Cathy Techtmann
County Treasurer	James S. Wall	Mark Gianunzio	Home Economist	Mary Burcalow-Kinney	Joanne Pihlaja
		Clara Maki, Deputy	4-H Youth Agent	(incorp. in other agent	Jillian Kirchhoff
Register of Deeds	Charles E. Paeske	Robert Traczyk		positions since 1922)	
		Danette Stephani, Deputy	Zoning Administrator	John Chayk	Gene Abelson
Coroner	Charles Gutekunst	Dr. D.J. Martinetti	Veteran's Officer	James Flandrena	Robert L. Morzenti
		Joseph Simonich, Deputy	Office of Emergency	Thomas Gamache	Thomas Olszewski
		Donald Pelkowski, Deputy	Government		
County Attorney/ Corporation Counsel	George Foster	David P. Morzenti	County Purchasing	Dan Reid	Louis Leoni

▲ Hurley, 1992. The 1992-94 Iron County Board of Supervisors. (l-r, sitting) John B. Chiapusio, Edward Borgi Borgiasz (Vice Chair), Louis P. Leoni (Chair), Eugene Calvetti, Richard L. Rowe, Milton Cayer, (l-r, standing) John R. Raabe, Doug Borcherdt, Carl Prosek, Thomas E. Popko, Jr., James H. Butterbrodt, Fred Lantta, Jr., Gary Ellis, James F. Strand. (not pictured: Kenneth P. Licht)

Lost Communities

Adequate natural resources and reliable transportation to move products and people were the building blocks of a community in Iron county. Some settlements failed to grow or faltered if either of these ingredients was missing.

Eager to sell land to new settlers, development companies mapped out communities like Pine Lake, Magnetic Center and Hoyt along rail lines on the bet that enough resource wealth would be found nearby to sustain industry and encourage settlement. When it was never found, all that these towns amounted to was a name on a plat. Ironton's fate as a bustling port city on Lake Superior was sealed when the railroad changed the terminus of its line to Bessemer. Other communities, like the sawmill towns of Emerson, Powell, and Kimball, did become thriving communities. Their bloom faded when the timber resources played out.

The story of VanBuskirk is a profile of a lost community. In 1886, the VanBuskirk Brothers established a sawmill six miles south of Hurley, adjacent to the East Branch of the Montreal River. By 1905 the mill was busy buzzing through the stands of white pine south of Hurley.

The Milwaukee Lake Shore and Western railroad brought logs to the mill and supplies and settlers to the new community that was growing up around it. Many of the newcomers were Finnish settlers with a dream to establish a family farm in the Cutover. Work in the mill provided a good source of insurance against financial ruin if crops failed.

It wasn't necessary to travel to the big city of Hurley, when thriving VanBuskirk had all that the settler needed. Three general stores, the VanBuskirk Cooperative, and two gas stations provided supplies for farm and home. Children attended the community's one-room school. Organizations like the Chapter of the Finnish Workers Federation, the Elo Temperance Society, and the VanBuskirk Cooperative Society added a social dimension to milltown and farm life.

By the turn of the century, the white pine was cut over. With its natural resource base depleted, the VanBuskirk mill closed in 1908. Workers and their families moved on to new opportunities. The lure of farming continued to attract settlers, but they were never numerous nor were the farms prosperous enough to support a business district.

Hardwood logging contractors continued to use the convenient siding at VanBuskirk, keeping it alive as a rail stop. About 1930, hardwood timber supplies began to dwindle and delivery of logs to the siding stopped. Today all that remains of VanBuskirk is a place name and the memories of the lumbermen and farmers who worked hard to make a living and a community there.

Iron County's Lost Communities

Town of Anderson
    Tyler Forks
    Moore
    Plummer
    Rouse
    Iron Center
    Potato Junction

Town of Gurney
    Curry

City of Hurley
    Germania

Town of Kimball
    Kimball
    Hinkle
    Meadville
    Fouche
    River Branch
    DeFer

Town of Knight
    Osborn

Town of Oma
    VanBuskirk
    Sandrock
    Magnetic Center
    Pine Lake
    Carson

Town of Pence
    Hamilton
    Hoyt

Town of Saxon
    Ironton

Town of Sherman
    Emerson
    Powell

County Municipalities

Kimball, c. 1900. Virtually, every community in Iron county started with a lumber camp like this operation. Note the "cookee" with his dinner horn at right and the barren hillside in the background.

Town of Anderson

Date Organized: March 14, 1900
First Chairperson: J. B. Anderson
Present Chairperson: Jean Pierrelee
First School: 1906
Population:
1910: 219
1920: 386
1930: 196
1940: 193
1950: 122
1960: 110
1970: 92
1980: 91
1990: 69

The Town of Anderson was created from portions of the Town of Knight and originally called the Town of Vogel. J. B. Anderson, a town pioneer, had been a member of the Ashland County Board and was instrumental in supporting the secession of Iron County from Ashland County in 1893. He also served as the town clerk of the Town of Knight until the creation of the Town of Vogel and was then elected its first chairperson. On June 7, 1903, the Iron County Board accepted a resolution to change the name of the town to Anderson in his honor.

Extensive logging operations were conducted in Anderson in the early 1900s. The Norman Brothers operated a sawmill in the community of Moore, but it was later moved to Gile. Roddis Line camps stretched into Anderson as far north as Lake O'Brien, connected by the Roddis Line logging railroad. Logging and lumber production is still a major industry in the town.

At the western end of the Penokee's extension into the county, Anderson has been the home of several sporting facilities and events including the Biathlon competitions at Camp Olympia developed as a year-round sports training facility, the start of the Paavo Nurmi Marathon, the Ullr Dag cross country ski race, the North Country Trail, and the White Cap Mountains downhill ski area.

Upson, 1985. Nordic ski racers stride away from the starting line at Weber Lake en route to the finish line in Hurley over the 26 kilometer Ullr Dag Race Course. The Ullr Dag was held in 1981 and 1985. It was well received by the racers who enjoyed the challenging terrain of the course which followed the Ullr Nordic across the rugged Penokee Mountains. The race was sponsored by the Penokee Rangers Cross Country Ski Club with assistance from the Hurley Holiday Inn and Haven North.

Upson, c. 1989. The White Cap Ski area built its new A-frame chalet in 1967 and continues to expand its downhill ski operations each year. The hill features a 400 foot vertical drop. New additions to the lodge and lodging facilities have made White Cap a major Midwestern ski area.

Upson, c. 1900. The Potato River has always been a favorite location for family get-a-ways. Upson Park on the Potato River in Anderson offers overnight camping, picnicking, a pavilion, and trout fishing, all next to beautiful Upson Falls.

Town of Carey

Date Organized: March 29, 1909
First Chairperson: L.M. Hardenburgh
Present Chairperson: Kenneth Otte
First School: South Carey School, built 1916-1917
Population:
1910: 1277
1920: 363
1930: 247
1940: 292
1950: 273
1960: 221
1970: 194
1980: 179
1990: 175

The Town of Carey was created from the remnant sections of the old Town of Vaughn, after it was parcelled off into other towns. The Town of Vaughn prior to the creation of Carey was the most irregular civil town, in terms of its boundaries, of any in Wisconsin. It was 16 miles long and 7 miles wide on the south. Eight single irregularily shaped sections made up the panhandle of the town to the north. Whereas most sections are one mile wide, the sections in the north varied between a skinny 1/2 mile to only 1/4 mile in width.

Large stands of pine, hardwoods, and softwoods were once found in Carey. Logging operations by the Montreal River Lumber Company (later, the Scott and Howe Lumber Company) began in 1886. Pine logging centered on the Island Lake area. The West Branch of the Montreal River, which flowed from the lake, was used to float logs to the company's mill in Gile.

Scott and Howe started logging hemlock and hardwood for its new Ironwood mill in 1916. Since water transportation was no longer feasible, the company extended rail lines south to Island Lake and back through the Town of Pence. The Island Lake area became a network of rail spurs and tote roads like the Camp 7 Road. Forty to fifty carloads of logs a day were taken out of the woods. Large logging camps, numbered 1 to 9, and Peterson's Camp, housed company loggers and jobbers.

Scott and Howe's operations in Carey halted in 1929 and by 1930 all of the logging railroad tracks had been torn up. These grades are now used as fire lanes and trails for all terrain vehicles and snowmobiles. Carey's water resources, like Island Lake and the Gile Flowage, attract outdoor recreationalists and vacation home owners.

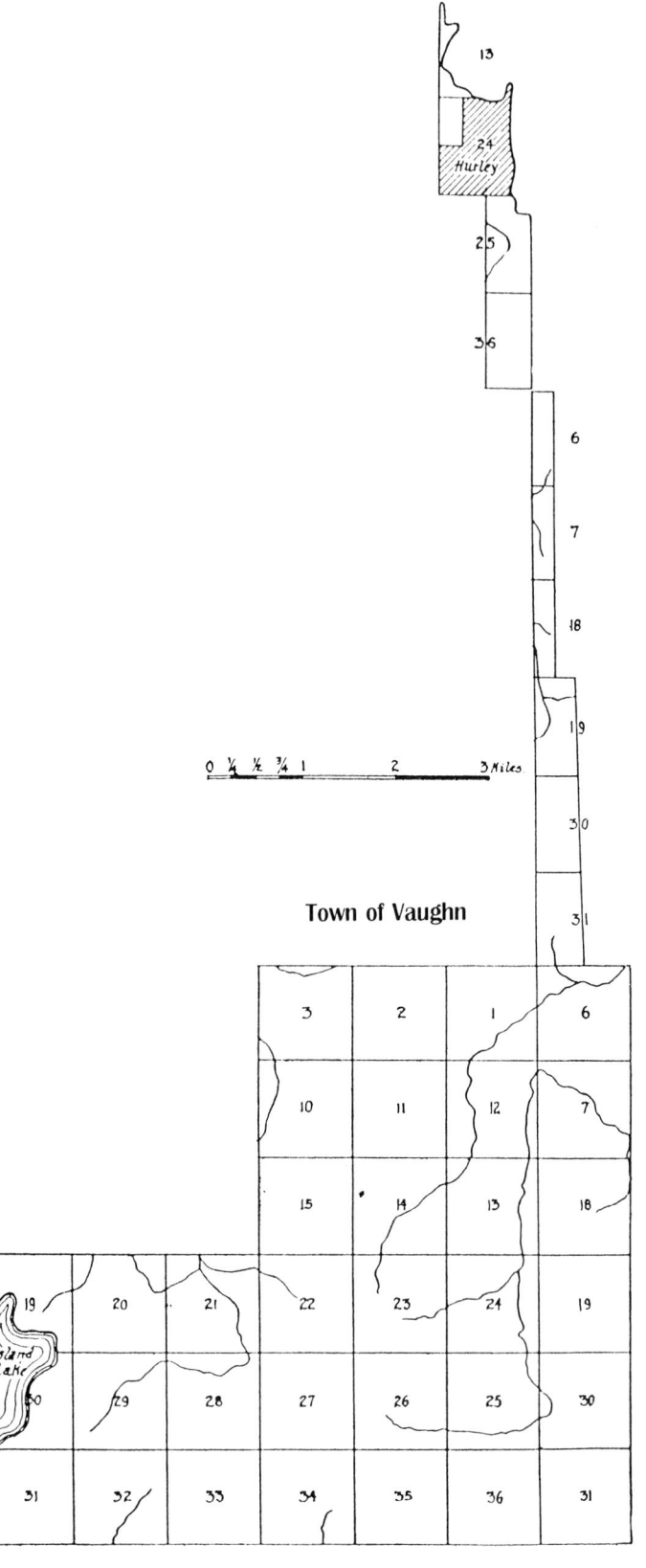

The boundaries of the Town of Vaughn were the most irregular of any civil township in Wisconsin. As other towns were organized, Vaughn was dissolved, renamed and reshaped into the Town of Carey.

Carey, c. 1919. The Carey Town Board prepares to take up town business in the town's new hall. (l-r) Mike Krall, town treasurer; Ed Hakala, town supervisor; Gust Kolu, town chairman; Matt Mattson, town supervisor; Arvid Nelson, town clerk. The town board had met at the Finnish Temperance Friends Association Hall from 1909 until the new hall was built in 1919.

Carey, 1965. Coxey's dairy farm was the only Grade A dairy in the Town of Carey. During the 1930s there were about 67 farmers in Carey, although most of them supplemented farm income with revenue from working in the mines, woods, or on government programs.

Island Lake, 1945. Val Gene and Shirley Coxey find an older growth tree that the loggers missed. The Island Lake area was extensively logged by the Roddis Company. In 1934 and 1935, Roddis extended their logging railroad north to Island Lake and Lake Six, where logging Camps 14 and 15 were established. Camp 15 was the last of the railroad logging camps. It closed in 1938 when the Roddis Mill in Park Falls suspended operations. Only one year's supply of timber remained around the camp and it was no longer feasible to keep it open.

Town of Gurney

Date Organized: April 25, 1914
First Chairperson: R.D. Hogan
Present Chairperson: Tom Innes
First School: c. 1914
Population:
1920: 216
1930: 237
1940: 185
1950: 161
1960: 129
1970: 135
1980: 153
1990: 143

The Town of Gurney was originally part of the Town of Saxon. On April 14, 1914 the town boards of the two communities met and agreed to divide the two towns. A financial settlement that compensated Gurney for the loss of $1016.46 in property in Saxon was agreed upon and the Town of Gurney was born.

Like many communities, the early history of Gurney was closely tied to logging. The first mill in town was constructed in 1897. It was enlarged in 1912 and its operation taken over by the Gurney Lumber Company. The company carried on extensive logging operations and employed as many as 200 men in the woods.

The Gurney Lumber Company was an innovative corporate citizen. Besides supplying employment, the Gurney Lumber Company's dynamo was used to generate electricity and lit up the community like a small city. The company operated a farm adjoining the mill site where they grew root crops, hay and oats for their work horses, and vegetables for their lumber camps. To keep isolated loggers happy, Gurney Lumber became the first company to show movies for the amusement of the lumberjacks. The tactic worked and was adopted at other logging camps.

The heyday of logging in Gurney ended in 1917 when the Gurney mill burned to the ground after being struck by lightning. Gone were jobs in the mill and woods, and electricity for the community. Logging jobbers continued to work out of the community. Many workers looked toward making a living off the land by farming.

Gurney, c. 1950. Potatoes were picked by hand at the Rowe Farm.

Gurney, c. 1991. A field of Atlantic potatoes on the VanderVeen Farm. During the 1991 season approximately 650 acres of potatoes were planted in Gurney. As logging operations around the community ceased, workers turned to farming. The area's light sandy soils and isolation from other potato growing areas make Gurney a good location to grow disease free potato stock. Certified seed potatoes from farms like the Swanee Superior Spud Farm and the Rowe family farms were shipped all over the country, making Gurney famous.

Gurney, c. 1990. Potato River Falls plunges 90 feet, making it the largest waterfall in Iron county. In 1938, the Mellen Granite Company made a second attempt to dam the river for power generation. Town Chairman W. C. Jensen admitted that a dam would mar the beauty of the falls, but supported the project on the grounds that the falls were inaccessible, that there were other waterfalls in the county and that the town needed the taxes. The Milwaukee Izaak Walton League began a campaign against the project and opposed any dam construction. The Public Service Commission's ruling against the project was hailed as a victory for conservation.

City of Hurley

Name: City of Hurley, formerly Town of Vaughn
Date Organized: April 1, 1918
First Mayor: Henry Meade
Present Mayor: Thomas Gamache
First School: 1886, established by Professor Charles Carna
First Church: 1886: St. Mary's of the Seven Dolors Catholic and First Presbyterian
Population:
1930: 3264
1940: 3275
1950: 3034
1960: 2763
1970: 2418
1980: 2015
1990: 1782

"Yes gentlemen, you heard right, there is such a town as Hurley and she is a mighty healthy two year old and don't you forget it. There are mines here and they have already yielded considerable good iron ore. Yes, there are churches and schools here. Of course, you have to pay taxes on your property and no insurance company has established an agent here yet where you can get insured for nothing. There are lots of chances here to make money, and you would not have to hunt very long to find places to lose it either, but if you are at all interested and want to know all about it, don't take anybody's word for it, but come and see." From an unidentified newspaper, c. 1886.

Hurley, 1991. Police Chief Ted Erspamer and Deputy City Clerk Elizabeth Aimone place the City of Hurley's seal on the wall of the new Hurley City Hall. The seal features Hurley's nightlife, snowmobiling, cross country skiing, and Paavo Nurmi Marathon highlighted in the center with an old fashioned street light bearing a street sign for "Silver Street." The new city hall offices were dedicated on December 14, 1991.

Hurley, c. 1930. The old Hurley City Hall. On June 3, 1944, after 54 years of service warning firemen from as far back as the great Klondike Theater fire of 1901 to the ringing of the 8:30 PM curfew, the Hurley fire bell was taken down. It is suggested that some civic organization make a monument to Hurley's history by placing the bell on a pedestal with the inscription, "With a desperate desire, and a resolute endeavor; Now, now, to sit forever."

HURLEY, 1886

Town of Kimball

Name: Named for A. M. Kimball, of the Kimball-Clark sawmill
Date Organized: April 1, 1913
First Chairperson: William Weber
Present Chairperson: Carl Prosek
First School: 1886
Population:
1920: 672
1930: 770
1940: 723
1950: 607
1960: 514
1970: 468
1980: 499
1990: 513

On September 23, 1886, C. R. Clark arrived with a party of men and women at Day's Siding. They had come by boat to Saxon and undoubtedly used the Flambeau Trail to take them overland to a site they could explore for mine holdings. Kimball's forest was so dense, it was said that the women had no use for clothes pins, since no breeze could penetrate the woods. Even the miners saw that Kimball's real wealth was in timber.

A sawmill, store and dwelling houses were erected by October. No sooner did the mill began humming, then fire struck and burned it and all of its timber supplies. It was rebuilt. The company became known for producing the finest matched hardwood flooring and even featured a boat building department. Wood products from Kimball were displayed at the 1893 Chicago World's Fair.

But the community would be revisited by fire. In 1903, a chimney fire destroyed a row of houses and the company store. Another, more disastrous fire, in 1904, burned the new mill, dry kiln, blacksmith shop, store, five homes, and about 3 million shingles. Once more the mill was rebuilt, only to be dismantled in 1920 when it was sold and moved to Gagen, Wisconsin.

Kimball, 1992. All that remains of the Kimball-Clark mill is the stone chimney of the drying kiln.

The Belmas Farm, 1930s. Neighbors working together, the Kimball threshing crew separates the oats from the chaff on the Belmas farm.

▲ The Into Finnish Athletic Club, c. 1930 (l-r), Bruno Ahonen, Telfield "Deppy" Ahonen, Hank Hamberg, John Hariu. Into typified the cooperative spirit of Kimball residents who worked and played together.

▶ Kimball Town Hall, 1960s. The town hall became the site of a Weinbrenner shoe factory that featured hand-sewn shoes and boots.

▼ Kimball Town Hall, 1960. The Kimball Trailblazers 4-H Club gathered at the town hall to board a bus for a trip to Bayfield and Madeleine Island. The club made an educational trip every year. The town hall once served as the Meadville school.

127

Town of Knight

Date Organized: April 19, 1892
First Chairperson: D. McVichie (Ashland County), Frank Logan (Iron County)
Present Chairperson: Fred Lantta, Jr.
First School: The Blue School, 1890
First Church: St. John's Finnish Church, c. 1900
Population:
1900: 1363
1910: 1259
1920: 901
1930: 762
1940: 698
1950: 518
1960: 417
1970: 324
1980: 294
1990: 265

The Town of Knight, together with the Towns of Saxon and Vaughn, were the three original municipalities that constituted Iron County when it split from Ashland County. The town was named for John K. Knight who may have influenced the military career of a young man named Douglas MacArthur. MacArthur's father had discouraged his son from going into the military since he was bitter from not receiving his own promotion after spending 28 years in service. Knight made a deal with the old soldier. If Colonel MacArthur would use his military influence to help Knight win a seat in the Senate, Knight would help young Douglas get an appointment to West Point. Knight never entered the senatorial race, but he persuaded his opponent to convince Milwaukee Congressman Theobald Otjen to make the appointment. Young Douglas probably didn't need a recommendation based on a political deal, since he scored a near perfect score on the Academy's entrance exam, but Knight had made good on his promise.

Iron Belt, c. 1910. Like many community pubs, Barto's Tavern sold more than spirits. Customers to Anna and Louis Barto's store could purchase fresh baked bread, Beech-nut tobacco, alarm clocks, or could enjoy an ice cream cone or phospate at their soda fountain.

▲ Iron Belt, c. 1910. The Iron Belt Opera House was the place to go when early settlers wanted entertainment. Productions such as the "Passion Play" and the "Face on the Barroom Floor" were dramatized in the theater located on the building's second floor. The lower level later became a silent movie theater, complete with the piano player who provided the film's musical score. The Trione Saloon is to the left of the Opera House.

▶ Iron Belt, c. 1920. Oscar Eilo, with the help of a very shaggy pony, prepares for the day's delivery of groceries from the Jackson Wiita Store. The Jackson and Wiita Store was among the largest department stores on the Range and stocked everything from farm implements to fine china. It provided grocery delivery service as far as Montreal and Pence.

Town of Mercer

Date Organized: 1908
First Chairperson: George Richardson
Present Chairperson: John Raabe
First School: Green School, 1894
First Church: First Methodist Episcopal
Population:
1910: 311
1920: 567
1930: 666
1940: 937
1950: 974
1960: 1048
1970: 1003
1980: 1425
1990: 1325

Mercer's location on a peninsula between three lakes has made it an important destination for travellers since the days of the Flambeau Trail. Its reputation as a tourist area has grown since the railroad brought the first newcomers to the community in 1894. Vacationers from cities like Chicago and Milwaukee travelled north on the Milwaukee Lake Shore and Western Railroad to spend summers at Mercer's resorts. Local folk from the Hurley and Ironwood areas built summer homes around the lakes. Summer camps, like Camp Keewatin, Camp Nokomis Girl's Camp, and Camp Roosevelt brought city kids north for a summer of fun at Mercer.

Mercer's northwoods and lake country ambiance continues to draw more tourists and second-home owners. Recreational activities have diversified to feature winter sports, especially snowmobiling. The purchase of the wild Turtle-Flambeau Flowage by the Department of Natural Resources in 1990 is expected to increase the number of tourists visiting Mercer, the "Loon Capital of the World."

Mercer, c. 1920. Camp Keewatin Academy on Echo Lake was more than a summer camp for boys. It was an institution of higher learning dedicated to, "work with the individual rather than the class and to give opportunity for outdoor life under the most favorable conditions. These make the Keewatin grad unique among his peers." Prep school courses were taught in regular academic work stressing reading, letter writing, penmanship, spelling and "mental arithmetic." The upper school prepared boys for university and offered courses in business, forestry, and agriculture. The Academy was only operated in Mercer until December 21st of each year, then students and teachers moved to warmer winter quarters on the east coast of Florida. Another educational summer camp was located between Spider and Oxbow Lakes. Called Camp Roosevelt, it provided education for 600 Chicago area boys for a 7-week session under the direction of the U.S. government non-commissioned officers, teachers, and counsellors.

Mercer, c. 1960. A group of girls from Camp Nokomis prepares for a canoe trip on Trude Lake.

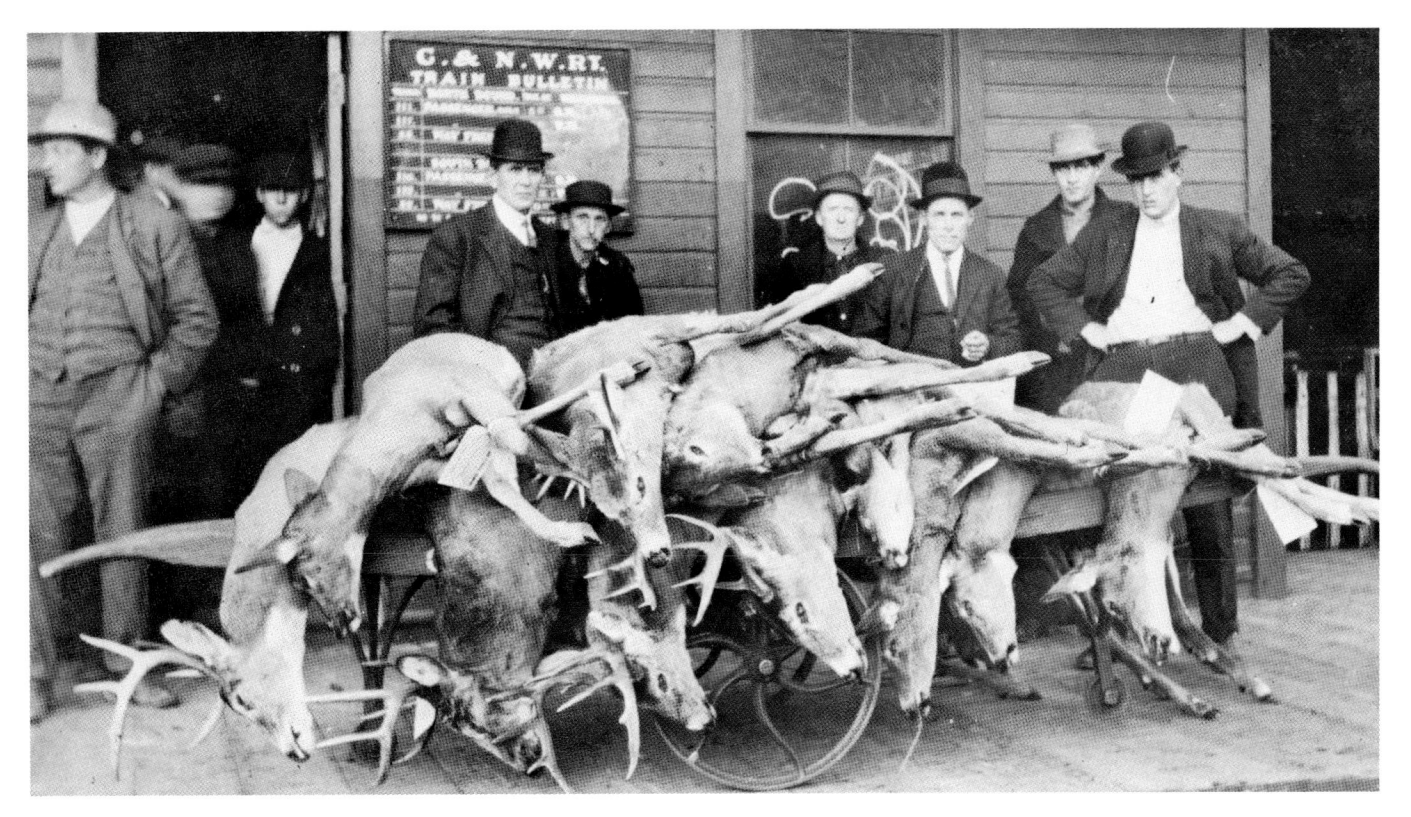

Mercer, 1910. A successful hunting party waits for the train to take their trophies back to the city. The rail depot was the hub of activity in Mercer. During the 1950s as many as 4 trains, 2 each way, and sometimes 2 freights, passed through the town.

Mercer, c. 1981. How much does a 16-foot loon weigh? The Mercer Loon which made its debut on May 22, 1981, weighs approximately 2000 pounds. It was erected at the location of the new Mercer Chamber of Commerce building to emphasize Mercer's claim as the "Loon Capital of the World."

City of Montreal

Name: City of Montreal, originally the Village of Hamilton
Date Organized: Incorporated as the Village of Hamilton on February 20, 1917; designated city of the fourth class by electors on April 1, 1924 and named Montreal.
First Chairperson: R. E. Robbins. First Mayor: John M. Price
Present Mayor: James Baron
First School: One-room school on top of Montreal Hill, 1894
First Church: Sacred Heart of Jesus Catholic, 1914
Population:
1920: 1890
1930: 1819
1940: 1699
1950: 1439
1960: 1361
1970: 877
1980: 887
1990: 838

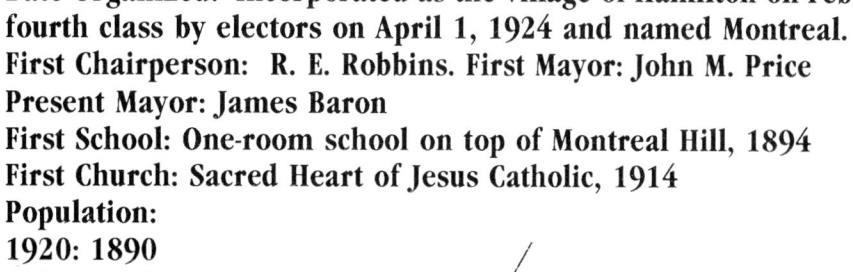

The basic A1 Style Ramsay home.

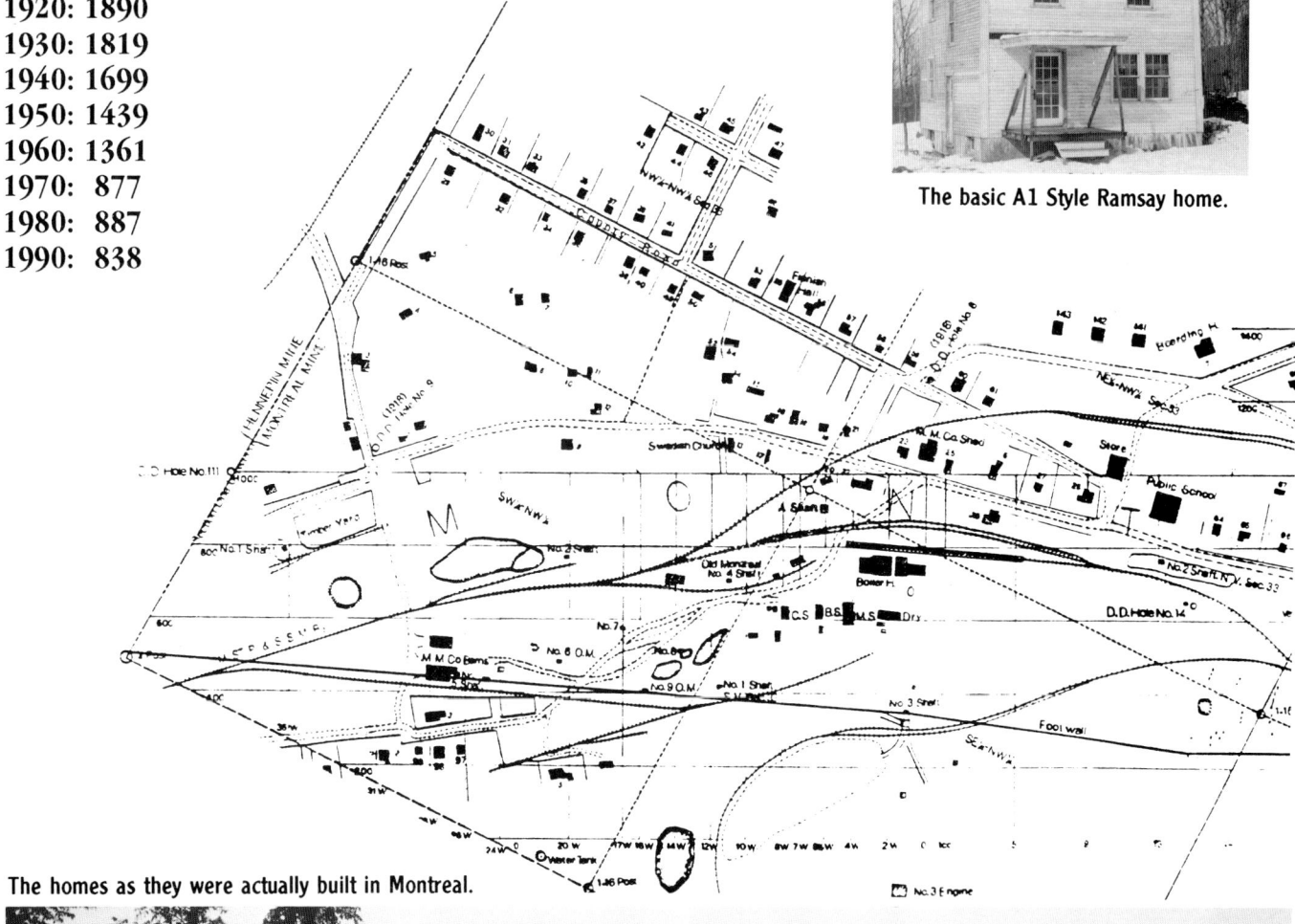

The homes as they were actually built in Montreal.

132

The mining community of Montreal epitomizes a planned company town--at its best. Investigations by mining companies proved that if workers were kept happy, production would remain stable and turnover rates would decrease. Nothing was taken for granted in planning Montreal. Housing reports for the Oglebay-Norton & Company in 1921 critiqued the design of other company communities, especially noting whether or not certain housing arrangements were conducive to the nationality and temperament of the miners. The home styles used in Ramsay, Michigan, were deemed most suitable. Pleasing architectural features that were incorporated into the original rectangular town plat were gently curving streets, playground and park areas, and careful arrangement of landscape plantings to give privacy and beauty to home and community.

The D2 Ramsay home used as the prototype for homes like the General Mining Superintendent's residence.

◄ The B2 Ramsay home had more space for families than the A1.
► The Hamilton Club opened in 1919 as a company-owned entertainment center for employees of the Montreal Mine and their families. It featured a recreation room with pool tables, billiards, a barber shop, soda fountain, kitchen, and stage. Movies were shown three times per week with other entertainment at other times. Montreal residents needed not to look any further than their backyard for good times.

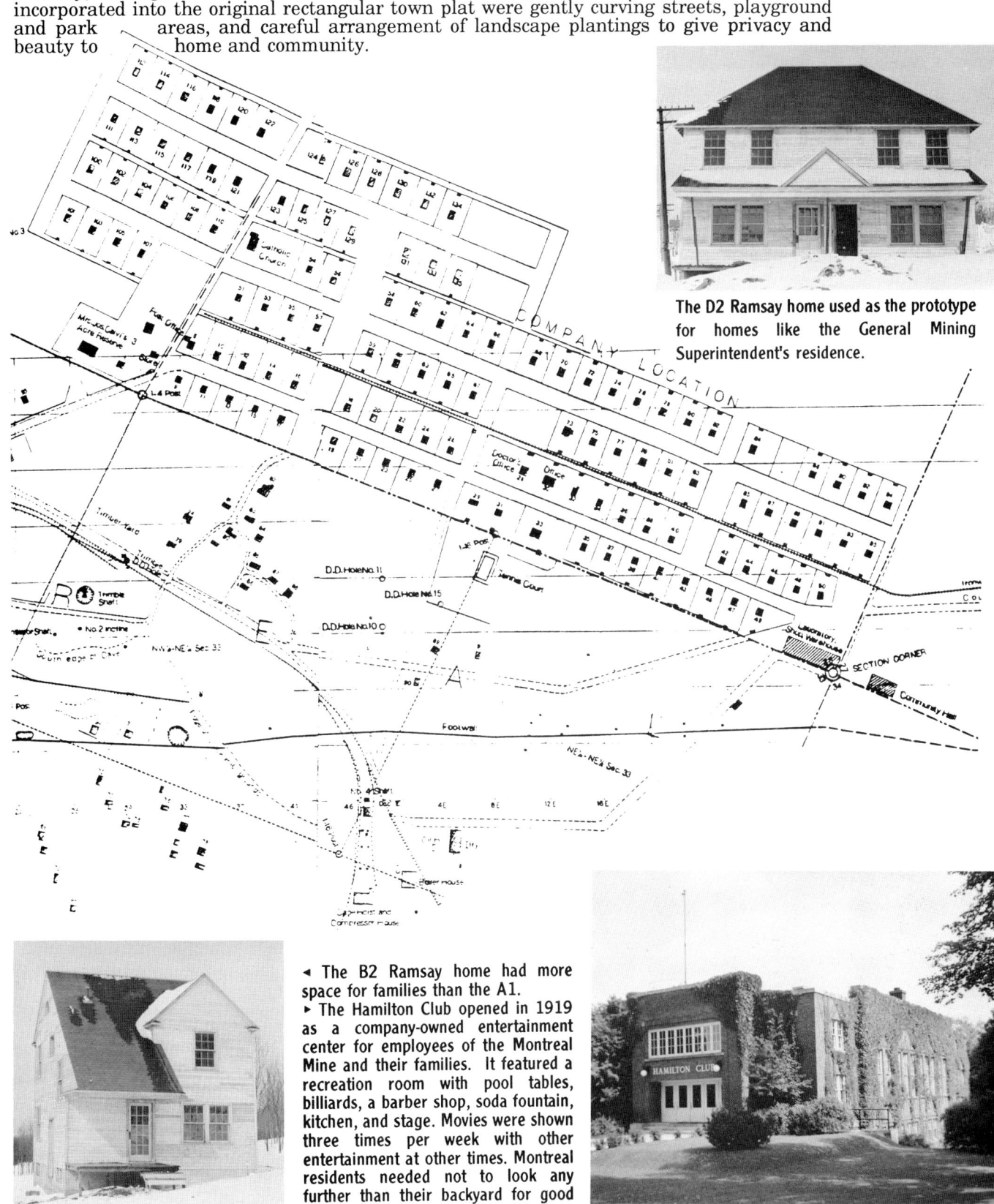

The City of Montreal is actually the combination of two communities, Montreal and Gile. These communities owe their separate origins to the separate resource bases upon which they were founded. Montreal was the site of the world's deepest iron ore mine. It produced over 45 million tons of hematite ore. Gile grew upon the white pine logs that fed the Montreal River Lumber Company mill. Even though the two sibling communities united in 1924, some disagreements were inevitable. In 1925, a disagreement on where to build a new school could only be solved by a compromise to build two schools, one in each town. To this day, the city of Montreal is the only community of its size with two post offices: one in Gile and one in Montreal.

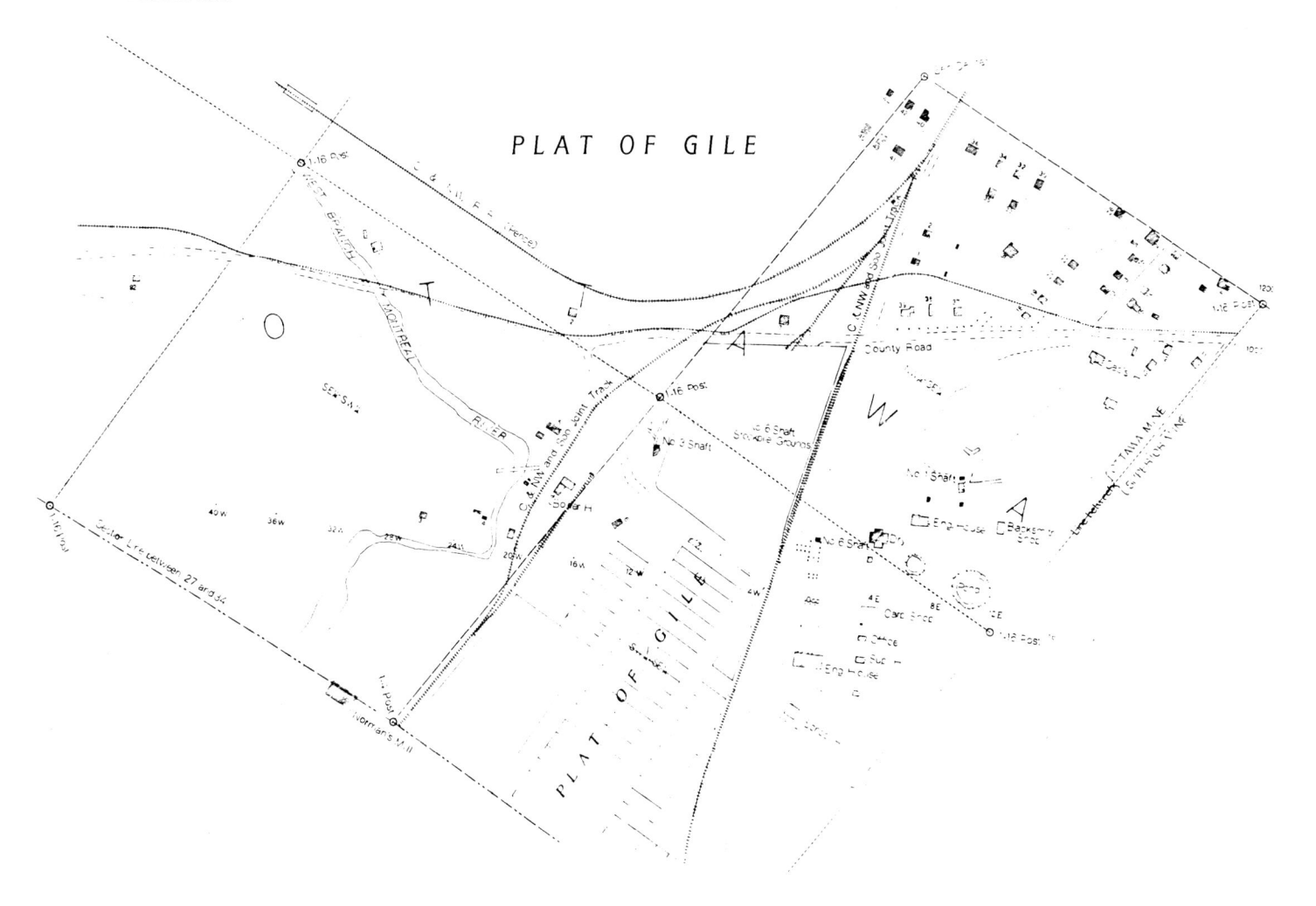

Gile, c.1900. East McCrossen Street. The street was named after Mike McCrossen who established the Montreal River Lumber Company in Gile.

134

Ross Siding, c. 1910. A "top loader" uses a peavey to steer a log into position on a flat car destined to deliver its load to the Montreal River Lumber Company in Gile. Logs were as important to Gile as iron ore was to Montreal.

Gile, 1890. The Montreal River Lumber Company, taken from the west bank of the Montreal River. The old company store is just to the right of the mill and the large building east of the store is the sleeping shanty. A large backup of logs is held in the West Branch of the Montreal by a dam at the mill.

Town of Oma

Date Organized: April 23, 1912
Origin of Name: Finnish for "Our Own"
First Settler: Thomas Hannula
First Town Chairman: John Rein
Present Town Chairman: Tom Davis
Population:
1920: 695
1930: 496
1940: 503
1950: 396
1960: 317
1970: 265
1980: 298
1990: 260

By the time the Town of Oma was created, two sawmills, at VanBuskirk and Sandrock, had already flourished and faded as its vast tracts of pine and hardwood were depleted. Yet, to Finnish settlers, this cutover land was special. It was a New Finland where, with a little bit of "sisu," they could carve a farm from the stumps and rocks, raise their families, and preserve their heritage.

But almost immediately, there was a glitch. The newly-formed town board could not agree on what to name their municipality. Story has it that one crusty oldtimer, who was not impressed with the speed at which town government seemed to be working on this issue, snorted out at a town meeting, "Oma Kaupunki" or "our own town!" With that declaration, he left for more pressing engagements, but "Oma" stuck as the name of the new town.

VanBuskirk, c. 1900. The VanBuskirk family home doubled as a bunkhouse for loggers employed at the VanBuskirk mill operations.

Oma, c. 1900. The Thompson Homestead was typical of the sturdy log buildings constructed by the Finnish settlers of Oma. This home was one of the first constructed along Old Highway 10. It is now the Kuduk residence. Finnish farmsteads, although not pretentious, followed the old country tradition of having many outbuildings. The barn was typically made of logs chinked with moss on the lower level, but left unchinked for ventilation in the hayloft. No homestead would be complete without a sauna with a lean-to woodshed.

Oma, c. 1900. Being out in the "back 40" took on a new meaning to those who frequented the Hidden Valley Bar in Oma. Although Oma's residents tended to live far apart from one another, the community had an active social life. Finnish-based organizations like the Finnish Workers Federation, the Elo Temperance Society, and VanBuskirk Cooperative Society offered a chance to meet neighbors and organize for the common good of the community. Groups like the Oma-South Carey Homemakers Club worked toward the betterment of family life through educational activities and community projects since 1920. The same spirit of cooperation unites Oma today.

VanBuskirk, c. 1935. There was no need to travel to the big city of Hurley, when everything that was needed for the farm or home could be found at VanBuskirk's three general stores and two gas stations. For those who wanted to go to Hurley for work or shopping, the Chicago & North Western Railroad made stops at Pine Lake and VanBuskirk.

Town of Pence

Name: Originally called the Town of Clement
Date Organized: May 7, 1923
First Chairperson: Clement Bertagnoli
Present Chairperson: Earl Brackett
Population:
1930: 418
1940: 454
1950: 371
1960: 314
1970: 234
1980: 191
1990: 181

Pence's early history could be called a trial by fire. During the early 1900s, Pence had an active Main Street with as many as seventeen bars, Ever's General Store, and several other businesses. On a cold January night, Charles Nyman, who had celebrated a bit too much in the Mozenier Saloon, is suspected of having knocked over a lamp or carelessly thrown a match. With no water on hand to fight the blaze, five other buildings plus the saloon were consumed. Again in the fall of 1910, a fire of unknown origin broke out and destroyed four more buildings. Town residents were helpless to fight the fire without water. Pence rebuilt part of its Main Street in brick after the fires, but fire protection was continually discussed at the meetings of the new town board. In 1931, for $1.00, the town purchased the old Montreal Springs. A pump station and water tank were also acquired. Fire hydrants now serve the entire town and residents enjoy a plentiful supply of water piped into their homes.

Pence, c. 1912. Friends from Pence and Montreal pose on one of the railroad trestles between the towns. (l-r, front row) Battista Baravetti, Louie Morgando, Chap Calvi, (middle) Barney Bertalone, (l-r, back row) Pete Mezzano, Eddie Cossette, Angelo Endrizzi, Don Reinerio, John Grasso. Edward Cossette would become the first Iron county serviceman to be killed in World War I while serving with the 32nd Division in Alsace on May 10, 1918.

Pence, January 11, 1910. Ashes were all that was left of Ever's General Store, Bertagnoli's Tavern, and the Reinerio Building after Pence's first big fire.

Pence, c. 1910. This new building was constructed of more fireproof brick after Pence's second major fire.

Town of Saxon

Date Organized: March 1, 1893, as part of Iron County.
First Chairperson: J. J. Defer
Present Chairperson: Robert Rowe
First School: 1897, at the old town hall
First Resident: 1865, Mr. Stahl
Population:
1900: 688
1910: 693
1920: 790
1930: 948
1940: 809
1950: 655
1960: 483
1970: 371
1980: 362
1990: 335

Saxon was one of the first three towns that comprised Iron County in 1893. Even before Iron County had been formed, Saxon was a booming logging and farming community. Early settlers even tried prospecting for copper, but economically feasible reserves were never found. The major settlement within the town was in the community of Dogwood, named like many of the sidings on the Milwaukee Lake Shore and Western rail line for a common northwoods tree. The name of the town was changed in 1892, when Depot Operator Grey felt that the name was undignified. His practice of yelling "sacks on" after he threw the mail sacks on the train seemed to fit the town. The town became known as Saxon.

Saxon, 1895. The Saxon charcoal kilns converted cordwood into charcoal for iron furnaces. Manuals like the "Handbook for a Homeseeker," published in 1895 to extol the virtues of settling northern Wisconsin, pointed out the advantages to farming up north over other areas. "The hardwood districts of northern Wisconsin stand in strong contrast with the plains region of the west. There the settler, no matter how much in need, must rely on one crop a year, be that what it may, for subsistence. Here, while clearing his farm from the woods, the settler sells wood to the charcoal burners, ties and telegraph poles to the railroad companies, and hardwood logs to the mills; thus he is sure of funds sufficient at least to meet immediate necessities of his family."

Saxon, 1902. The Saxon Union Train Station. The tracks of two railroads, the Milwaukee Lake Shore and Western and the Duluth South Shore and Atlantic, crossed at Saxon. Seeing a mutual benefit in cooperation, both railroads agreed to operate a union station that would handle freight and passengers from both lines. A crossover track was also constructed in case either one of the lines had a major catastrophe, the other track could be used.

Saxon. c. 1990. The sandy loam and red clay soils of Saxon combined with the moderating effects of Lake Superior on the local climate, encourage dairy farming. Farming reached its peak around 1938, when there were 138 farms, mostly dairy operations, in Saxon. Dairy farming remains a locally important industry in the area.

Town of Sherman

Date Organized: April 19, 1907
First Chairperson: D. W. Emerson
Present Chairperson: Edward Borgi Borgiasz
First School: Maggie Murphy School-1910
First Residents: Bernhard and Lulu Pripps
Population:
1910: 73
1920: 183
1930: 110
1940: 189
1950: 164
1960: 153
1970: 152
1980: 336
1990: 267

The Town of Sherman was originally named Emerson in honor of its first town chair and the man that established the Emerson Sawmill. Brothers David and John Emerson in 1905 incorporated the Emerson Land Company for the purpose of buying and selling timber and farm lands. The brothers were attracted to the area to salvage a large stand of white and red pine they owned that had been blown down in a tornado. Mill machinery was brought in, loggers and families moved in, and camp buildings were erected. Almost a solid stand of old growth hemlock, maple, yellow birch and some white pine stretched out toward Park Falls and Powell. Tragedy struck the Emersons in 1909, when three members of the family, including John Emerson, were struck and killed by lightning. The family operation was never the same and the mill closed. The name of the town was changed to Sherman in honor of the town's second chairman William Sherman.

Springstead, c. 1920. Almost all of the pioneer settlers around Springstead capitalized on their lakeshore locations by starting resort businesses. One of the first pioneers to do so was Mr. Watrous of Chicago who operated a semi-private resort at Springstead Lake around 1905. Since there were no roads or railroads into Springstead then, guests would have to endure a ride over rough "corduroy" roads in a wagon or buggy during the summer months.

Springstead, c. 1920. Seifert's Glenwood Resort on French Lake in Powell offered its guests a hotel in a commodious, frame structure, good meals from the ice house larder of meats, competent guides adept at preparing the noonday shore lunch, and speedy relief from hay fever.

Emerson, c. 1910. The Emerson School was one of the earliest schools in Sherman.

Springstead, 1964. The red brick Springstead School was built around 1937. (l-r, front row) Melvin Marsh, Stephan Johnson, Gary Kessler, Robbie Pripps, Stanley Robbins, (l-r, second row) Cleora Larson, Nancy Johnson, Ralph Meyer, Rita Visser, Karen Johnson, Peggy Marsh, (l-r, third row) Barbara Larson, Donald Streigel, Phillip Walker, Kenny Meyer, James Johnson, Linda Morrill, (l-r, fourth row) Arvilla Losby, cook, Gail Haiden, teacher. Children were taken to and from school in family station wagons turned "school buses" from 1960-1964 after Mr. Visser discontinued regular bus service.

143

The Lake Superior bluffs near the mouth of the Montreal River, 1852. The first published depiction of an Iron county scene appears in D.D. Owen's "Geological Survey of Wisconsin."

1688
- First mention of the Montreal River on a French map. Probably named for the mountainous site of Montreal, Canada on the bluffs of the St. Lawrence River.

1774
- The Iron county area annexed to the Province of Quebec by the English.

1820
- The territorial survey party led by Lewis Cass arrives at the mouth of the Montreal River and finds an Indian settlement there.

1824
- American Fur Company operates a trading post at the mouth of the Montreal.

1837
- January 26: Congress establishes the state boundary line of Wisconsin as the headwaters of the Menominee River and the Montreal River.

1841
- Government surveyor Captain Thomas Cram incorrectly identifies the headwaters of the Montreal River as the point where a small tributary meets the East Branch of the Montreal River and incorrectly establishes the Wisconsin/Michigan border. The error gives Wisconsin the Penokee iron mining district around Hurley.

1843
- The Chippewa are forced to cede their land in Wisconsin; the Chequamegon Bay area is open for settlement by non-Indian peoples.

1847
- William A. Burt surveys the Wisconsin state line. Burt's new invention, the solar compass, proves invaluable in tracing the line because an ordinary compass is severely affected by iron in the soil.
- Surveyor D.D. Owen camps near a copper mine at the upper falls of the Montreal River.

1848
- The State of Wisconsin is admitted to the Union.

1850
- Charles Whittlesey conducts a geologic survey of northern Wisconsin. He learns the Chippewa word for iron, "pewabic," and so names the hills extending into Iron county. However, he misspells the word on his official survey maps as "penokee."

1857
- The Panic of '57 halts mining speculation in the Saxon Harbor area. Plans to develop the village of Ironton as a mining hub and terminus for a great rail line, linking Lake Superior with central Wisconsin, are scrapped.

1858
- Professor J.A. Latham, a University of Wisconsin geologist who walked the Range, reports the presence of iron ore in the Gogebic Range area. His reports go largely unheeded.

1861
- The Civil War begins.

1862
- Public lands sold at annual auctions for a minimum bid of $1.25 per acre cause huge tracts of northern Wisconsin land to be obtained by out-of-state investors and in-state speculators.

1865
- April 9: The Civil War ends.
- Mr. Stahl is given 20 acres of military land in the Saxon area under the provision that veterans of wars could claim government land for their service.

1870
- Northern Wisconsin lumber is in demand as orders for wood products of all kinds boom after the Civil War.

1871
- While on a survey of the Upper Peninsula, geologists T. B. Brooks and Raphael Pumpelly trace an iron formation across the Montreal River into Michigan.

1879
- First discovery of a commercial iron ore body on the Penokee/Gogebic Range is made by Richard Langford, a trapper. He notices chunks of red ore in the roots of an overturned tree while crossing a hill south of Bessemer.
- A group of men representing the Lake Superior Ship Canal Railroad Company work a tract of land on the west side of the Montreal River and find abundant iron ore.
- The Iron Boom begins. Thousands of prospectors flock to Hurley and new mining camps open every day.

1880
- The saying "Hurley, Hayward, Cumberland and Hell," the four toughest places on earth, is used to refer to the boisterous, lusty days of the 1880s.

1882
- J.O. Hayes and his brother, E.A. Hayes from Ashland, team up with mining explorer Nathaniel Moore and confirm extensive bodies of iron ore west of the Montreal River, waiting to be taken out.

1883
- The Colby Mine in Bessemer opens. Upon hearing of the new iron ore discoveries of the Range, the terminus of the Milwaukee Lake Shore and Western Railroad is changed from Ontonagon to Bessemer.

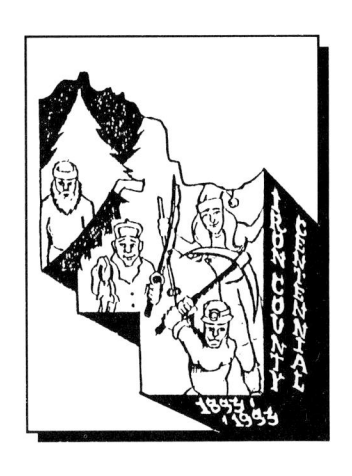

Iron County Chronicle

1884
- A village site is platted by Northern Chief Mining Company. It is named in honor of Michael Angelo "Glen" Hurley, a prominent Wausau attorney who is a partner in the company and interested in development on the Range. It is referred to as "Glen" Hurley until 1886 when the "glen" is dropped.
- Hurley boasts of two well-defined thoroughfares: Silver Street and Copper Street. The surrounding area is so thickly wooded, woodsmen lose their way within a short distance of town limits.
- The Hayes brothers lease the property that will become the Germania Mine. They ship the first mining machinery to Hurley--a boiler and pump--from Ashland to Mellen by train and then overland by ox cart at the breakneck pace of 2 miles per day!
- Montreal Mining Company is organized under the management of Oglebay Norton & Co. of Cleveland. Hematite ore will be found within their properties by 1885.
- October: The Milwaukee Lake Shore & Western Railroad reaches Hurley and Ironwood. The railroad refuses to acknowledge the existence of Hurley and only delivers passengers and freight as far as Bessemer. By 1885, traffic is so heavy that Hurley is made a stop.
- H. Surprise builds the first building in Hurley, a small shanty, near the corner of 5th Avenue and Silver Street.
- Northern Chief Iron Company is formed with capital stock of $3 million divided into 30,000 shares at $1.00 each.

1885
- A building lot is presented as a gift to the first baby born in Hurley, Miss Edith Thomas.
- April: Mr. Swanson and friends walk from Iron River Michigan, to Hurley to strip surface earth at the Germania Mine. They find the much discussed boom town's Main Street to be really a "snake trail boasting of only four buildings along its entire length."
- May 15: The first ore is mined from an open pit at the Germania Mine.
- Summer: Railroad link from Hurley to the new ore docks in Ashland is completed, providing an economical method of transporting iron ore via ships to mills on the lower Great Lakes.
- July 13: 15 carloads from the Germania Mine carry the first ore from the Penokee-Gogebic Range shipped out of Ashland.
- First death in Hurley is believed to be that of Mr. Whitefield, son of a wealthy New York family, who was sent "out west" to rid himself of his wild habits. Not finding it possible to change his habits in a town like Hurley, he takes his life.
- October 1: First newspaper, the Montreal River Miner, is established by Messr. Gowdey and Goodell.
- The Penokee Railroad Company completes the difficult connection across the Penokee Range linking Hurley with Mellen.
- Dan McCrossen starts the Montreal River Lumber Company at Gile.
- Iron Exchange Bank is chartered on November 26 with assets of $5,000.
- Duluth, South Shore and Atlantic Railroad is complete across northern Iron county.

1886
- May 8: First issue of the Gogebic Iron Tribune, editor F.A. Hand. On the development of Hurley, the Tribune opines: "Each day, a new building goes up and the woods resound with the crash of falling trees and the music of a saw and hammers."
- A second industrial boom-logging! Sawmills are built by Mead, McLaughlin and Company in Hurley and the VanBuskirk Brothers 6 miles south of Hurley.
- The Montreal River Lumber Company starts the first logging operations in the Town of Carey. It is estimated

that 2,000 "wood choppers" are at work on the Range.
- Mining is booming! The number of mining corporations has grown to 87 with aggregate capital stock of $105,000,000, up from only 3 corporations with stock of $1,105,000 in 1885!
- May: First school is organized in Hurley by Professor C.H. Carna. By June, a School Board has organized and classes are being conducted in a local building consisting of two departments and about 100 pupils presided over by Patrick Lennon and Miss Nellie Nicholson.
- September: A party of men and women prospectors, led by C.R. Clark travel from Saxon Harbor to "Day's Siding" (later known as Kimball).
- September: The dry house at the Germania Mine is destroyed by fire. Nearly all the miners lose their clothes, a loss of about $300.
- October 19: Grand Opening of the Burton House! From the diary of John Burton: "Grand day of it, fine weather, fine feeling. At Hurley, Cornet Band was playing as train came in and 1,000 people gathered. Governor and myself were ordered to take arms and head the procession behind band to hotel. Got up from the banquet at 3:30 a.m."
- November 6: "Every day new exploring camps were fitted out and the woods were 'fairly alive' with men all intent on striking something."

1887
- The Iron Mining Boom Busts! Hurley faces depression. January: A petition signed by 800 Hurley taxpayers to create the County of Mills from Ashland County is sent to the state legislature. Opposition from Ashland newspapers and politicians is immediate.
- March: The bill creating the county of Mills passes the state assembly. Senator George Merrill, Ashland, lobbies against it. Local newspapers charge that Ashland county seeks to hold on to the Range to keep its tax base.
- March 17, Montreal River Miner: "According to the estimate of pine standing in Michigan and Wisconsin, made by A.G. VanSchaick, it will take about 200 years to saw it."
- April: Germania miners strike after having to wait for their pay.
- June 27: A disastrous fire starts in the Gogebic Meat and Provision Company's rendering department destroys all buildings between 2nd and 3rd Avenues on Silver Street.
- July 9: A second Hurley fire more devastating than the first starts in the scenery of the Alcazar Variety Theater. The fire sweeps through the building so rapidly that ten people perish. The fire spreads eastward over the previously burned downtown area, destroying the entire business district on Silver St. as far as 5th Ave.
- Sept. 17: A fire destroys most of the business district of neighboring Ironwood, Michigan.
- First Finnish miners arrive to work at the Montreal mine.

1888
- July 12, Gogebic Iron Tribune: "In July of this year, 1888, the mosquitos are so bad in the woods that work in some of the mills had to be abandoned until the annoyance was removed by a chance of weather or providential interference."

1889
- July 4: 120 guests are registered at the Burton House. Fashionable carriages line the streets of Hurley, and wealthy businessmen ride their private railway cars here to conduct business affairs.
- September 21: The Iron Exchange Bank is robbed of mining payroll of $25,180 in bank notes and $13,980 in gold. $2,560 in silver is left by the robbers, supposedly because it was too heavy to carry.
- Work starts on the Milwaukee Lake Shore & Western connection to Mercer from Lac du Flambeau.
- There are 4 passenger trains each way on the Milwaukee Lake Shore & Western and two over the Wisconsin Central each day through Hurley.

1890
- March: Fire at the Germania Mine destroys No. 2 shaft, and five miners suffocate. All shafts are closed until May to smother the fire.
- Hurley and Ironwood merchants enter into an agreement that stores in both places are to be closed on Sundays.
- May: Hurley's First National Bank opens for business.
- A variety of schools spring up in Hurley. Father Gilbert erects a Catholic school, a German teacher starts a school at the Lutheran Church to teach German, Miss Summers offers an evening class in writing, and Mrs. Hayes Chynoweth offers a school featuring a literary society and oratory debates for the workers at the Germania Mine.

1891
- September 3: Town of Vaughn Board ordains that "it shall be unlawful for horses to run at large... and any owners thereof shall be liable to a penalty not to exceed $10 for each and every occasion."

1892
- April 19: Town of Knight established as part of county of Ashland.
- May 13: Voters of Town of Vaughn adopt a resolution to build the first Hurley Free High School.
- Village of Dogwood renamed Saxon, from the phrase "Sacks On" used by Depotmaster Grey to signify that he had thrown the mail sacks on the train.
- The street railway from Carey to Bessemer is built. It is estimated that a single car running between Hurley and Gile transports 1,100 people a day
- The Sharey Zedek Jewish Temple is organized in Hurley.

1893
- March 1: Iron county, is created by an act of the Wisconsin legislature, and adopted on March 3.
- Local mines close and depression hits the Range during the nationwide "Panic of 1893." Wisconsin Governor Peck comes to Hurley by train with carloads of relief supplies donated from all parts of the state.
- April 6: First marriage recorded in Iron county: William Hanley and Catherine Meyers.
- April 17: Albert Gribble is the first recorded birth in Iron county.
- May 22: First recorded death in Iron county is Mary Webb.
- June 9: First class of graduates from Hurley Free High School. The class motto selected by the 6 female graduates: "Perseverance Wins Success."
- First county Superintendent of Schools, Kathleen Nicholson, is appointed.
- The unique matched style of hardwood flooring produced at the Kimball-Clark Mill of Kimball is exhibited at the World's Fair.
- Pence is platted and will remain an unincorporated village belonging to the Village of Montreal until 1917.

1894
- January 13, Montreal River Miner: "Hurley businesses meet to find a way to get poor men to work for their provisions to avoid the humiliating and demoralizing effect

of supporting men in idleness."
- April 3: The Town of Vaughn sells its Town Hall to Iron County for $32,000.
- June 8: William H. Bridgeman publishes the first issue of Iron County Republican newspaper. It will be merged with the Montreal River Miner in 1903.
- First school building is erected in Montreal on top of Montreal Hill.
- Mercer School is built under the supervision of Charles Moffett. First teachers are Fannie Folsom and "The Belle of Mercer," Annie Weber.
- First through train service to Mercer.

1895
- October: The "Speranza," an Italian fraternal society, is organized in Pence.
- Iron county's 83 farms produce a total of $33,322 in agricultural commodities this year.
- The Finnish temperance society "Valon Kipina" is organized in Iron Belt.

1896
- 400 men are now employed at the Montreal Mine.
- Mining halts at the Pence mine.

1897
- March 7: John Burton sells the Burton House Hotel for $23,000 in postal stamps plus $7,000 in cash to a Mr. Ross. The stamps and envelopes that change hands in the deal weigh over two tons.
- April 12: Town of Vaughn levies a poll tax upon every male inhabitant between the ages of 21 and 50, except all disabled soldiers who served in the late war, firemen, paupers, idiots, and lunatics.
- First lumber mill is built in the Town of Gurney.

1898
- First school at Manitowish is built.
- Sawmill at Sandrock is built, but abandoned by 1918.

1899
- Carrie Schwartz is the first white child born in Mercer.
- Kimball-Clark Mill in Kimball burns down for the first time.

1900
- County Population: 6,600.
- March 2: An ordinance presented to the county Board by D.C. Bennett creates the Town of Montreal.
- Town of Knight releases some of its western territory to create the Town of Vogel. It will be renamed the Town of Anderson in 1903.
- Barney Pripps' sawmill is the first to operate in Town of Sherman.

1901
- March: Three miners are killed and one is buried alive but later rescued during a heavy fall of capping at the Atlantic Mine in Iron Belt.
- A fire that starts in the Klondike Theater building almost consumes all of Hurley's Silver Street.

1902
- "It was no easy journey, especially for a wife and four children, over a ragged logging road and a narrow brush-hidden trail to the $400 quarter section," Matti Kivi, upon leaving mining in Ironwood to farm in north Hurley.

1903
- April: Chimney fire in Kimball destroys a row of homes and leaves 37 families roofless.
- The "Roddis Line," a network of logging camps connected by rail line to the new Roddis mill in Park Falls, is constructed. Operations continue until 1947.
- Smith and Daley Sawmill in Iron Belt offers a monthly paycheck to its workers of $30 for 26 days of labor at 10 hours per day.

1904
- January 3: Frank Marta publishes the Italian newspaper, "La Nostra Terra" ("Our Land"). It will be renamed the Iron County News in 1913 and will merge with the Montreal River Miner in 1950.
- July: Kimball-Clark Mill in Kimball burns down for the second time; fire takes 3,000,000 shingles, several homes and businesses. The mill is rebuilt for a third time.

1905
- George Richardson builds The Northern Hotel in Mercer.
- Mercer train depot burns down.

1906
- July 15: The red sandstone cornerstone of St. Mary's Catholic Church in Hurley is laid.
- A socialist union local is organized in Iron Belt.

1907
- April 19: Town of Emerson is created from the southern portion of the Town of Vaughn and named after its first town chairman, D.W. Emerson. It will be renamed the Town of Sherman in 1918.
- The Michigan legislature authorizes Peter White to lobby the Wisconsin legislature to correct Captain Cram's 1841 survey of state boundaries. White finds an unfavorable political climate and decides to take up the issue at another time. That time never comes. One week after he leaves Madison, White drops dead.
- A corporation called the Agricultural National League of Iron County, or "Agricola," is formed to lease land to Italian tenant farmers in Kimball's "Dago Valley."

1908
- Town of Mercer is created from the Town of Vaughn.
- Old Manitowish school burns and is replaced by a new school located in the heart of village's pine grove.
- The iron miners' day averages 9.76 hours long with pay at $2.44 per day or 25¢ per hour.

1909
- High demand for lumber means lots of activity in the logging camps. Good wages, $30 - $35 per month.
- March 29, 1909: Town of Carey is created.
- June 25: Disastrous fire destroys the Scott and Howe Lumber Company Mill in Ironwood. It is rebuilt in 1910 with a capacity of 150,000 board feet of lumber per day.
- June: The Mercer "Pineknots" baseball team prepares for the upcoming season.
- Epidemic of typhoid sweeps through Mercer.

1910
- County population: 8,306.

1911
- January: Fire consumes five buildings in Pence and takes the life of Charles Nyman.
- Windsor Mine dry is blown up by intentionally set dynamite. One miner is killed, five others severely injured.

- A socialist union local is organized by Finnish settlers in VanBuskirk/South Carey.
- A drive of cedar logs to Park Falls is the last river drive on the Flambeau River.
- August 11: The longest baseball game ever played on the Gogebic Range, the Cary Empires vs. the Ironwood Tigers, is started at 2:15 PM and ends after 21 innings at 6:10 PM. The Empires win by 2 runs.
- October 23: The Hurley post office is designated a postal savings bank to discourage the hoarding of large sums of money by foreign-born people unfamiliar with U.S. banking systems and who send large sums to Europe.

1912
- Gurney Lumber Company, one of the largest on the Range, expands its mill.
- Iron mining ceases in the Town of Knight.
- April 23: Town of Oma is established.
- Saxon Falls dam is built to produce hydroelectricity.
- Operations at the Germania Mine cease due to lack of demand for ore.

1913
- F.A. Emunson buys the Iron County Publishing Company and with it the newspaper "La Nostra Terra." Emunson renames the paper the "Iron County News."
- In the last decade, Iron county shows the greatest increase in land values of any county in northern Wisconsin, rising from $5.14 to $16.25 per acre.
- February 5: Hurley Library officially opens with 700 books contributed by Hurley residents.
- May: Fire starts in an overheated stove in Hill's store and destroys eight buildings in Iron Belt.
- August 23: Census of the Joint District #1 of the Towns of Vaughn, Cary and Montreal finds 1,649 school age children.
- September 25: The J.J. Defer Store in Saxon is again destroyed by fire. On the number of fires that have visited Saxon, the Iron County News reports that "as of late, it is thought that some ill-minded person has been the cause of a great many of them."
- September 27, Iron County News: "The scarcity of houses to rent in Hurley and people looking for places... would seem to indicate that Hurley is as good as any place on the map."

1914
- January: Carey opens a new 2-story brick school house, with steam heat.
- April 25: Town of Gurney is created by mutual agreement and monetary settlement between Gurney and Town of Saxon.
- September 19: The long-distance telephone service connected from Hurley and Ironwood to Manitowish and Mercer.
- Electricity from the Gurney Lumber Company provides Gurney with residential electricity and streetlights.
- New brick schools open in Mercer and Saxon.
- A legislative committee meets in Hurley to consider developing a state forest reserve in the Towns of Emerson and Mercer and parts of Forest, Oneida, Vilas, and Price Counties.

1915
- March 13: Judge Risjord rules in favor of Silver Street property owners and Northern Chief Mine against an assessment by the Town of Vaughn to fund brick paving for Silver Street. Two-thirds of the property owners eventually do contribute to the assessment.
- October: A second fire sweeps through Pence, destroying four buildings and some residences.
- November: The new Iron Belt Telephone Company brings phone service to Town of Knight.

1916
- Tornadoes rip through the Long Lake area.
- October 10: "It has been brought to our attention that women of lascivious behavior...have become inmates of places in the Village of Hurley. Resolved by the Town of Vaughn to take such steps as necessary to cause all such women and keepers of places harboring them or permitting their resorting to be prosecuted."
- Charles Comiskey, owner of the White Sox, builds a summer retreat for his team on Trude Lake in Mercer and calls it the Jerome Hunting & Fishing Club.
- LaJoyce School in Kimball is constructed.
- Scott and Howe Lumber Company logs hardwood and hemlock near Island Lake.
- The Gurney Lumber Company shows motion pictures in camps to keep lumberjacks from leaving. It is a huge success.

1917
- February 20: The community of Montreal is incorporated as the "Village of Hamilton."
- April 4: United States enters into World War I.
- July 29: Miners Strike Across Range! "The workers themselves know that it is the best time to break the iron chain that binds us to the ground." Demands include pay of $6.00 per day for 6 hours work, abolition of the contract system, abolition of blacklisting miners, and $4.00 for 8 hours of work for surface workers.
- Superior Falls dam is built to produce hydroelectricity.

1918
- An influenza outbreak becomes serious despite precautions forbidding public meetings and closing schools. 10 deaths are reported.
- January 4: Fire breaks out in a Hurley bakery and rapidly spreads to Massucco & Martinetti, Getz, Longhini buildings and the Sacchetti shoe repair shop. Losses estimated at $35,000.
- February: The Hurley Community Civic Club appeals to the town board and district attorney to enforce the state's Sunday saloon closing law, but the club gets no action. Hurley saloons are finally closed on Sundays for the first time in history by order of the Attorney General and the Governor.
- New Settlers Cooperative Creamery Association of Hurley ships first 700 pounds of butter to markets in Chicago.
- Boundaries of the Town of Carey are changed, giving sections of the Town to Hurley, Kimball, and Montreal.
- August: A fire caused by lightning destroys the Gurney Lumber Company Mill, ending the lumber era in Gurney.
- November 11: World War I ends.
- Food Prices: Flour, $2.85 @ 49 lbs.; Sugar, 9¢ lb. Butter, 48¢ lb. Cheese, 30¢ lb. Potatoes, $1.65 @ 100 lbs.

1919
- Kimball-Clark Mill is sold, dismantled, and moved.
- American Legion Edward L. Cossette Post No. 58, is organized in Hurley, and named after the first Iron county man killed in World War I.
- The Hurley Commercial Club is organized.
- July: Over 200 cars are parked on Hurley's streets as customers purchase spirits on the eve of prohibition. Local papers report that there is enough booze stored in Hurley and Ironwood to "float a battleship."

- July: The Hamilton Club opens for the entertainment of employees of the Montreal Mine and their families.
- October: Uncle Sam orders Hurley "bone dry." 55 Hurley saloon keepers are notified that the sale of 2½% beer, wines, and "kicking" ginger ale will not be permitted. Even all beer signs must be taken down.

1920
- County population: 10,261; the all time high.
- January 19: Prohibition is enacted.
- March: The Hurley National Bank opens and reports deposits of $86,000 on the first day of business.
- March: Two men dressed as lumberjacks hit Town of Carey Treasurer William West over the head, take his gun and $1300 in town tax money.
- Presbyterians found Camp Galilee, near Mellen, as a non-denominational church camp.
- Lake Lavina is eliminated as a source of municipal water for Hurley due to high bacteria counts. Price of water obtained from Ironwood may be raised from 3.75 to 20.7 cents per 1000 gallons.
- December 29: Deputy U.S. Marshal William Pugh and federal lawmen raid Hurley and arrest 57 saloon operators for violation of prohibition laws.
- Oma-Soca (South Carey) Homemakers Club initiated, sponsored by the Iron county Agriculture Extension Office. It is officially organized by 1924 under the creed: "We homemakers believe in the sanctity of the Home, the cradle of character, blessed by motherly devotion and guarded by fatherly protection."

1921
- Dan Shaffer is hired as the county's first Extension Agent.
- May 16: Free mail delivery service starts in Hurley.
- July: Fred Wilke is the first conservation warden in Iron county.
- The large brick Iron Belt School opens, consolidating three smaller Town of Knight schools.
- October 10: A large "booze" caravan from Milwaukee to Hurley is stopped near Woodruff by federal marshalls. In the ensuing gun battle, John Chiapusio is fatally shot and two other Hurley men arrested for illegal transportation of liquor.

1922
- The Hurley American Legion Auxiliary Post is chartered.
- Iron county is the eighth county in Wisconsin to be classified as free of tuberculosis in its cattle herds.
- 10,000 pounds of dynamite are used to clear county farms of cutover stumps as part of a land clearing program of the Extension Office.
- Most of the iron mines on the Range are now electrified.
- May 7: The County Board approves two county parks: one at Mercer and the other at the end of the road leading from Saxon to Lake Superior.

1923
- February: A blizzard isolates Hurley for two days as extreme cold and snow prevent trains from arriving.
- April 23: Federal Judge Claude Luse dismisses the case against 57 Hurley saloon operators arrested for violations of the prohibition laws.
- May: Telephone poles are removed from Silver Street in Hurley.
- May 7: Town of Clement is created from Town of Montreal, but later renamed Town of "Pence."
- July 27: Health care examiners are startled to find a large percentage of underweight children appearing at Free Chest Clinic in Hurley.
- A one-room school building in Kimball is constructed to replace the Hinkle School. The Pence School opens.
- A two-year closed deer season for Iron county is considered since the total kill in the county was only 136 deer last season.
- A road linking the Town of Sherman to Park Falls is constructed and paid for, in part, by Park Falls merchants.
- The final attempt by Michigan to "claim" the Hurley area, based on the 1840 survey error by Captain Cram, is finally settled in favor of Wisconsin.

1924
- April 1: The status of Montreal is changed from a village to a City of the Fourth Class.
- May: The body of Andrew Sigler, a Hurley cafe and restaurant owner, is found along Hwy. 51.
- June: Andrew Gudleski, a worker at the New Central Saloon, confesses to the killing of Andrew Sigler and claims Mrs. Sigler hired him to do so. She later claims she shot her husband in self defense. Mrs. Emma Sigler is convicted and becomes the second woman in Wisconsin's history to be sentenced to life imprisonment.
- July 12: Iron county's first farmers' market opens at the foot of 3rd Avenue and Silver Street.
- The Plummer Mine in the Town of Pence permanently ceases operations. The headframe is not dismantled and today remains the last standing headframe in Wisconsin.

1925
- The brick Mercer Town Hall is built.
- An exceptionally dry summer causes a fire to break out at Rice Lake near Mercer. Whipped by 60 MPH winds, the fire threatens Mercer. Town Chairman Ed Evenson orders the entire town closed and all men to fight the fire. Favorable winds narrowly spare the town. The fire is stopped only when it enters a swampy area near Spider Lake. 4,000 acres are burned.
- Disagreement between Gile and Montreal as where to build a new school results in two schools being built, a 2-room school in Gile and the 12-room Roosevelt School at the foot of Bourne Hill in Montreal. Both open in 1926.
- September: Six Hurley saloons are padlocked for one year following violations of the prohibition law.

1926
- May: Rural Route #1 is established for the Hurley area, serving 140 families. Tovio Sunie will deliver mail with his Ford touring car.
- Iron county ranks second among Wisconsin counties in amount of timber cut: 2 billion board feet per year.
- The 16,966 acre Turtle-Flambeau Flowage is created by a dam at the junction of the Turtle and Flambeau Rivers.
- 29 Hurley saloons are padlocked to stop flow of moonshine after two undercover federal marshals disguised as lumberjacks find it easy to get a drink.

1927
- The thin fertility of Iron county's forest soils requires farmers to begin liming to get good crop production.

1928
- Mercer Ranger Station built under leadership of V.A. Moon.
- Camp Roosevelt, a Chicago school system camp run by the U.S. government, opens on Spider and Oxbow Lakes near Mercer, providing summer training for 600 boys taught by 75 non-commissioned officers and teachers.
- Snowfall on the Range for 1927-28 is 207.9 inches, 48.9 of which fell in April.

1929
- July 19: The "old pesthouse" which was used as the City Poorhouse burns down. Occupants escape safely but lose most of their clothes.
- Walter Cisewski, a Montreal high school senior, wins the title of the World's Fastest Typist. He types 104 words per minute for five minutes with no errors.
- Town of Sherman hall is erected.
- Scott and Howe Logging Company operations cease in the Town of Carey; the timber is completely cut over except for a few crooked trees.
- Mercer's Hotel Northern burns down.
- April: A tornado strikes the Mercer and Sandrock area, demolishing several buildings on the Popko farm and three steel power transmission towers.
- October 29: The stock market collapses, marking the beginning of the Great Depression.

1930
- Iron county feels the burden of increasing tax delinquencies as cutover land is abandoned and the depression deepens. The new county Conservation Committee, working with county Agent E.H. Dietz, begins a survey of all tax delinquent land and agrees to put those lands not suited for agriculture aside as forest reserves.
- The federal government asks to include in a new federal forest a large portion of southern Iron county which is nearly deforested and unsuitable for agriculture.
- September: 6.7% of Iron county's population of 9,933 people are unemployed, the highest unemployment rate of any Wisconsin county.
- December 19: The Hurley school board adopts a teacher contract clause stating that "in the event that any female teacher shall become married during the term of her contract, the contract... shall terminate at the date of her marriage."

1931
- March: The Iron Exchange Bank installs bullet-proof glass partitions, armored steel plates, and electrically-charged steel spikes to prevent robbers access to the bank room. Small portholes in the armored plates will allow bank employees to fire guns at robbers who may be in the lobby.
- Town of Pence purchases the old Montreal Springs, giving the town a reliable source of water for residential and fire protection.

Mercer, c. 1935. Conservation Department personnel stock fingerling walleye and pike in local lakes.

1932
- February 6: The Northland Sports Club holds another successful Winter Carnival featuring a mammoth parade, a masquerade ball, skiing, skating, hockey and tobogganing at their Lake Lavina clubhouse.
- June 24: Hurley National Bank becomes the fourth bank on the Range to suspend business to protect the money of its depositors.
- September 30, 12:03 AM: After 41 years, Lake Superior District Power Company ends streetcar service. The final run is a gala event. However, the over-enthusiastic "mourners" blow the whistle so much that there is not enough air pressure to get the streetcar to the car barn.
- October 2: The majority of Hurley's Italian Societies merge into a new organization called the "Italo-Americano."
- The Iron County Board establishes the first 5-county forest units from 80,000 acres of tax-delinquent land.

1933
- January 1: The Iron County Forest is officially born when the Wisconsin Conservation Department approves the county's first entry of land into the County Forest Program.
- U.S. 2 from the Ashland county line to Hurley is concreted, replacing old Highway 10.
- June: 40 young men from the county, selected for service in the Civilian Conservation Corps, are given a rousing military send-off from Hurley.
- June: All mines on the Range are now closed down.
- June 25: Company 660, CCC Camp Mercer at Manitowish opens with a force of 215 men.
- August: Wages for Roddis Company logging camp woods workers are $.27 per hour for a 48-hour week.
- December 24: Camp Upson Civilian Conservation Corps Camp Company 1609 opens.

1934
- March 8: Iron becomes the third county in Wisconsin to create "Forestry and Recreation District" zones where settlement is prohibited.
- April 22: John Dillinger and several members of his gang outwit federal agents at Little Bohemia Lodge.
- Important projects in the development of the county forest system begin: section corner marking, tree planting, signing, and securing an assistant to the county agent to conduct forestry work.
- South Carey School closes.
- Cary Mine resumes operations.

1935
- Iron county's assessed valuation of $10,029,620 is $276,333 less than in 1934.
- February: The WPA Education Program is initiated to reduce illiteracy, strengthen home and family life, safeguard the welfare of young children, naturalize aliens and instill the American spirit. By 1937, 79 county residents attain citizenship.
- Mercer Fish Hatchery is built at Lake of the Falls by donated labor and contributions of citizens.
- September 12: The County Board accepts a quit claim deed from Richard Schomberg Jr. to create an 80-acre park at Layman's Creek to be called "Schomberg" Park.
- Iron Belt gets a WPA sewer and water project to safeguard public health by improving its water supply and sewerage disposal facilities.
- The state approves an extension of the Northern Highlands State Forest into parts of the Towns of Mercer and Sherman.
- The Roddis Lumber Company builds "Camp 15," the last of its logging camps, near Moose and Island Lakes.

1936
- February: 380 school children in towns of Mercer, Saxon, VanBuskirk, Iron Belt, and Sherman begin receiving WPA hot lunches.
- Iron county is classified as one of 37 drought-stricken counties. The federal Agriculture Conservation Program (ACP) begins in response.
- July 12: Temperatures reach a record 104°, climaxing the worst heat wave on record. Six deaths are attributed to the heat.
- A scarlet fever epidemic, the worst epidemic since the outbreak of influenza in 1918, sweeps Iron county, resulting in 80 cases, but no deaths. Schools are closed for two weeks.
- Iron county's first Forest Ranger, John Morris, is employed to check on county lands, timber cutting, land sales, and corner surveying.
- November: Mercer Community Hall, built of 80-90 foot long Norway pine logs by WPA-employed Finnish craftsman, nears completion. No power equipment, chinking, nails, or spikes are used in construction.
- Saxon Consumers Cooperative Association is organized.

1937
- Mercer Fish Hatchery produces more than 6 million walleye and muskies.
- Strong demand for ore opens mines again, boosting miner's wages to $6-$8 per day for underground work.
- The Saxon School District leases 120 acres of land on the south shore of Weber Lake and establishes a school forest to teach conservation to high school students.
- September: 500 people are employed in WPA work projects in the county.

1938
- "Iron County History" is compiled from newspapers, records, and other sources by the Iron County WPA Historic Project #6555, a branch of the Women's and Professional Projects sponsored by Hurley Joint School District #1. This document becomes the definitive collection of Iron county history.
- January 25: The worst blizzard ever to hit Iron county brings drifts of snow 15 to 20 feet high and over 40 MPH winds. Silver Street "looks like no man's land." Mines are closed, and milk supplies run short.
- "Our timber is nearly gone. Land that once produced a rich source of revenue is now denuded and, worse than that, in almost every instance is tax exempt. There is little use for this cutover land in such vast quantities with even the best of agricultural commodities... so that owners have stopped paying taxes entirely, forcing counties to take title to enormous acreage" reads the 1938 assessors report for Iron county.

1939
- June 23: A severe hail storm drops stones as large as hen eggs. Thousands of dollars in crop damage are reported. Not a single neon sign in the Hurley/Ironwood business district survives.
- June 25: The Oglebay Norton Company pays 95% of total taxes in the City of Montreal. Of the 400 homes in Montreal, 140 neat frame buildings are owned by the company and rented to miners at $1.50 per room per month. They are repainted white every 5 years on the outside and redecorated inside at the company's expense.
- The first stumpage revenue of $678.78 is generated from the new Iron County Forest.

1940
- County population: 10,049.
- Hurley Schools open 2 weeks late due to an epidemic of infantile paralysis.
- Cornerstone at new St. Mary's parochial school in Hurley is laid on the day President Roosevelt set aside for prayer that this country may remain at peace, "while the rest of the world has been at war for almost two years."
- Construction of County C requires that the old Hurley Cemetery at the junction with Highway 77 be moved. The first bodies to be buried in the old cemetery, which was used from 1885-1890, were those of T. McConnell who died of pneumonia, W.H. Whitefield of suicide, James Pierson of delirium, and A. Beariblund of fever.

1941
- April: The gates of the new Gile Dam closed today on the West Branch of the Montreal River and will flood approximately 4 square miles in Pence, Carey, and Montreal.
- December 7: Pearl Harbor is attacked. On December 8, the United States declares war against the Axis powers.
- The fireplace at Whispering Pines Resort, outside of Mercer, believed to be the largest fireplace in the world, is featured in Ripley's Believe It or Not.

1942
- The Hurley Joint School District considers a shortened school year to release some 1,200 boys and girls from school two weeks early for agriculture and defense work.
- January: Iron County Courthouse employees pledge themselves to the defense of their country through the purchase of defense savings stamps.
- February 1: A Montreal youth is believed to be the first Iron county fatality of World War II. Adam (Woit) Woitkielewicz died on his 25th birthday while serving with the U. S. Navy in the Pacific.
- February: The Town of Mercer is the first in the county in contributions to the Badger Bomber Drive.
- Hurley has a new industry, Walter Meyer Sausages.
- "We are waiting for the Japs to try us again." Message from Pvt. Fino Constantini, located at Fort Kamehameha in Hawaii, near the area bombed by the Japanese on December 7.
- A Pence lad, 2nd Lt. George Bertagnoli, sights Axis subs while flying from Cuba to Puerto Rico and Trinidad.

Mercer, c. 1940. Collecting cones for replanting in state and county forests.

•April: Thieves strip tires from a car in the first tire theft in the county since tire rationing began.
•August: Special state beverage tax division agents, along with FBI men, swoop down on Silver Street. In only 20 minutes, they clean up the "bright" light district and incarcerate 17 men and 34 women.
•Seven Hurley taverns must close to keep the license quota at 78.

1943
•Lt. Fred Harries of Hurley, son of Rev. and Mrs. C.L. Harries, is awarded the Distinguished Flying Cross.
•June 25: Iron and Gogebic Counties cooperate in the first black-out test.
•December: A Hurley club owner is fined $25 after pleading guilty of violating the city ordinance which forbids the playing of music by a Victrola, piano, or other musical instrument where liquor is sold.

1944
•Among area families who have five or more sons serving in the armed forces are the Matt Secor family and the Thomas Gamache family.
•February: First Lt. Lloyd Thompson, 27, of Mercer recently chalked up his 25th bombing mission against Nazi Europe as a bombardier aboard a Flying Fortress.
•August 13: Hurley city employees meet and take initial steps to form a union of city workers.
•The Town of Kimball has the distinction of having a husband and wife serving in the armed forces: Cpl. Toivo Pelto and Pvt. Julianna Pelto.
•First Lt. David Rautio of Hurley is Awarded the Distinguished Flying Cross.
•Staff Sergeant Earl Barncard, Mercer, while on a volunteer scouting mission during the capture of Manila, kills 15 Japanese snipers, three of them after he was wounded. His bravery enables his company to destroy a strongly fortified enemy position. His stealth is attributed to lessons learned in Iron county's woods.

1945
•January: David Secor of Hurley has the bad luck of being on two U.S. warships, the West Virginia and Ward, that are sunk. He is reported to be safe and well.
•A vagrant was arrested in Hurley and was given a 60-day sentence, the first 10 days will be on a bread and water diet.
•May 7: Germany surrenders in World War II.
•"We are sorry, but due to the meat shortage, we are unable to make enough pasties for sale to take out. We hope to be able to sell them by the bagful soon." Daoust Pasty Shop.
•August 6: The first atomic bomb is dropped on Hiroshima, Japan. A second is dropped on Nagasaki on August 9. Japan surrenders on September 2, 1945.

1946
•July: Due to the congestion and increased traffic, Hurley city officials erect a four-way stop sign at 2nd Avenue and Silver Street.
•August: Hurley city workmen start pulling up the brick on Silver Street in preparation for blacktop.
•August 24-25: A homecoming celebration for area servicemen and women is held, sponsored by the American Legion and V.F.W. organizations.
•September: Hurley sells 292,000 bricks for $7,767.45.

1947
•February: Despite the notoriety of being fireproof, an aging neglected Burton House Hotel burns to the ground.

•October 6: A meeting is held to organize an Iron County Tavernkeepers Association to promote goodwill, citing tavernkeepers being "constantly criticized and attacked by groups wishing to put our businesses out of the way."
•October 24: Extremely dry weather causes an explosion of fires across the North. The Iron Belt fire, where 5,000 acres of cutover land had burned, is now under control. Firefighters try experimental seeding of clouds with dry ice to produce rain clouds without success.
•A downtown revitalization boom sweeps Hurley and new storefronts are installed on several businesses.
•October: New transmitter towers for WJMS are erected south of the Cary Mine.

1948
•January 11: Hurley is threatened with running out of water when water levels on Lake Lavina drop due to low rain and snow. If there is a severe freeze, water could be cut off completely. However, the prospect of not getting enough freezing weather to make ice is considered more of an emergency. "Hurley without ice is more unthinkable than Hurley without water. Without ice, there can be no highballs, and a good deal of the city's commerce on Silver Street could be paralyzed." Montreal River Miner.
•August 5: Robert Sohl, son of Dr. and Mrs. Baird, wins heats in the 200-meter Olympic breaststroke competition in London. Sohl attended Hurley High School.
•August 6: The Hurley Chamber of Commerce is given a rock "core" from the new Cary Mine shaft. The favored place to display it is on the southern approach to Hurley on the "triangle" just south of the Memorial Building. Officials are still pondering how to move it to its new location.

1949
•March: The Hurley Midgets basketball team wins the State Championship! 10,000 people and a 300-car caravan turn out to welcome the team back home.
•June: The Hurley Chamber of Commerce proposes that everything paintable on Silver Street--buildings, lamp posts, bridges--be painted silver. Three businessmen respond and paint their buildings red.
•Attempts to find a new municipal water supply on the Canalia farm northwest of Hurley yield disappointing results. The time has come for city officials to work out a contract with Ironwood to furnish the 200,000 gallons per day needed by the city.
•July 4: Over the holiday weekend, heavy rains cause flooding of the Montreal River.
•October 18: A cyclone damages half of the roofs in Iron county and uproots many trees.
•October 26: Twenty four sections surrounding the Turtle-Flambeau Flowage are detached from the Town of Sherman and added to the Town of Mercer by action of the Iron County Board at the request of Sherman.
•November 11: 800 miners end their 7th week on strike against U.S. Steel and return to work at the Cary and Montreal Mines.
•December 1: Declared "Airport Day," the first airline and airmail service on the Range begins at the Gogebic Airport via Wisconsin Central Airlines.

1950
•County population: 8,714.
•April 7: The first issue of the consolidated Iron County News and Montreal River Miner, now called the Iron County Miner, is off the press.
•April 28: Mercer pitches in to build a home for Dr. Henry Ashe to provide Mercer with a permanent doctor.

- June 25: The "Korean War" begins. An armistice is signed on July 27, 1953.
- September: Better mail service for the Hurley area appears imminent with the news that the evening Flambeau Train #216 will carry mail.
- Thanksgiving Day: Fire causes $150,000 in damage to a Hurley building on the corner of 1st and Silver, which housed the Showboat Club, Club Fiesta, and the Magic Bar.

1951
- June 18: A fire at the Cary Mine idles more than 300 men. As of June 29, the fire is still being fought. Miners return to work on July 2.
- August 4: The Mercer/Winchester Road is dedicated. Reigning as the beauty queen of the dedication ceremonies is Alberta Seifert of Springstead.

1952
- June 2: Miners Strike! In Iron county, 1,000 men are affected by the Cary and Montreal strikers. The strike will end by August 1.
- The Hurley School District reports that it is "free of debt" for the month of June, except for its "current and ordinary bills."
- November: The "ice man" is now a thing of the past as John Bino, Sr. hangs up his ice tongs, marking the end of the Interstate Ice Company.

1953
- February: Hurley city officials learn that refrigerated beer can be sold in stores and markets.
- May: H.A. DeRosso, Carey resident and graduate of the Hurley High School, who sold his first western story in 1941, publishes "Under The Burning Sky" in this month's issue of Colliers Magazine.
- September: A "welcome home" reception is held for Sgt. Harry Brunelle of Gile, who was a prisoner of war for 29 months.

1954
- February 9: The Jones & Laughlin Steel Corporation is granted exploration rights and the option to lease county lands to the east of Pine Lake. It is speculated that they are exploring for taconite ore in the highly magnetic "anomaly" between Pine Lake and Lake Evelyn, first discovered by the Kissinger Mining Company in 1886.
- The Veteran's Addition and Erspamer Addition are added as new residential areas in Hurley to accommodate new home demands by returning servicemen.
- June 6: First issue of the Mercer News is published, sponsored by the Joint Council of Mercer Organizations, editor Ella K. Beierle.
- October: The section of the world's largest crude oil pipeline passing through Iron county is under construction. When completed, it will be able to transport 86,000 barrels of oil per day on a 635-mile journey from oil fields in Edmonton, Alberta to refineries in Sarnia, Ontario.

1955
- April 11: J.E. Murphy, Superintendent of the Hurley Schools for 48 years, tenders his resignation after a serious illness. June 25, 1955 is designated "J.E. Murphy Day" in his honor.
- The highest year of production at the Cary Mine, 684,809 tons shipped.
- June: The state starts action to close seven Hurley taverns: the French Casino, Hi-Ho Bar, Riverside Bar, Doll House Tavern, Frenchy's Bar, Flame Bar, and Blackhawk Bar, on charges that the establishments are nuisances and "a menace to the morals of the community."

- July 1: Iron county is informed that the U.S. Navy has named a Land Ship Tank (LST) the USS Iron County-LST 840. An LST is described as a boxey ship that can steam right up on shore on its flat bottom and "disembowel" itself of tanks and troops.
- November 2: 20% of Hurley taverns face closings. Padlocking and license suspensions are ordered.

1956
- The Roddis Company sells all its lands.
- March: Paul's Store in Hurley has grand opening located at the site of the former Range Theater.
- April: Two 12-year-old girls are in the state spelling bee at Madison: Helen Bowers, Oma, and Kathleen Curik, Hurley.
- All Iron county tavern operators, food handlers, and their employees are required to have x-rays taken to certify they are free of tuberculosis.
- August 28: Fire destroys the Keith Jesse Sawmill, Mercer's main industry.
- The Hurley High School begins behind-the-wheel training in automotive driving. Watch out pedestrians!
- Simpson Electric Co., a division of the American Gauge Machine Co., Chicago, locates in Mercer.
- October 4: Dial telephone service comes to Saxon.

1957
- The electorate of the Town of Knight votes to dissolve the Iron Belt School and to send their 40 students to the Hurley Schools. 25 students from Manitowish are presently being bused to the Hurley High School.
- April: Historical Society is started in Mercer. Mercer citizens, under the leadership of W.S. Carow, will compile an historical book about their town.
- July 10-12: Hurley "Whiteway Days" are held to formally dedicate the new whiteway lights on Silver Street.
- Hurley Police Department installs a mobile radio system.
- October 28: A 12 lb., 15½ oz. baby girl is born at Grand View Hospital in Ironwood and is believed to be the biggest baby born there to date. Her name is Sally Rae daughter of Mr. and Mrs. Buckley Peterson, Upson.

1958
- The Hurley School Board orders the closing of the Pence and Montreal schools.
- May 20: A carelessly extinguished campfire, causes a fire and burns 1,000 acres near Beaver Creek Flowage.
- July 14: Tornado causes extensive damage to downtown Mercer. Iron county is declared a disaster area.
- The federal government authorizes $433,500 to improve Saxon Harbor.
- November 14 headline: "Safecrackers Hit Iron County Treasurer's Office. $50 Stolen From Vault."
- Iron county has 172,000 acres of land under forest crop control - the third largest in the state.

1959
- Kindergarten class formed at Mercer School.
- Two vacated school buildings, Montreal and Pence, were placed up for sale by the Hurley School Board.
- Iron county's first nursing home, Sky View, opens.

1960
- County population: 7830.
- January 24: Open house day for the new Kimball Community Center.
- February: The Oma School District petitions to join the Hurley district.
- March 17: In the race for April's Presidential primary

election, Senator John F. Kennedy visits the Hurley area.
- April: Found inscribed on a 2" x 6" rafter of the old Paul store building when it is razed: "Douns he was sick yesterday. Mable is sick and Myrtle is working in her place. Sam Rautio is selling tickets. I wonder if I will be working in this store when this is taken down. Nit."
- May: The Iron County Forestry Committe accepts a $4,775 bid from Dr. R.C. Patterson of Stoughton, Wisconsin for 170 acres of land in the Weber Lake area of Iron Belt, and approves a 50-year lease for an additional 200 acres for the development of a ski resort. Groundbreaking for the future Whitecap Mountain Ski Area takes place on May 25.

1961
- February: Four Air Force fliers are killed as their jet bomber crashes between the Gile Flowage and Island Lake.
- May: Second Plane Crashes! An Air Force B-47 bomber crashes eight miles southwest of Hurley. Of the four persons aboard, two survive. Game Warden Warren Holger is among the first to discover and rescue the survivors.
- October: The Town of Saxon is the site of the 20th Century Fox film, "Adventures of a Young Man," starring Paul Newman, Jessica Tandy, Eli Wallach, Michael Pollard, and Ricardo Montalban.
- November: A Hurley minister, Rev. Edward Ketcham, urges local taverns to be lawful. He described the city's legal limit of 78 tavern licenses as "ridiculous for a city of 2,900 people." There are 56 taverns in operation.

1962
- June 15: Job qualifications for stenographer position at the Iron county Nurse's Office include that the applicant "must be unmarried."
- August 10: Iron ore production at the Montreal Mine officially stops.
- December: Hurley telephone numbers will consist of the "561" prefix followed by four more numbers to conform to a national telephone numbering system.

1963
- Mercer organizes a VFW post.
- Iron County Supervisors select a section of Boston Park on top of Germania Hill as the site of a new county courthouse to cost $480,000. Plans for the building are dropped following the receipt of a letter from the Cary Mine Union objecting to its erection.
- June: A feasibility study to develop greater recreational opportunities by damming Alder Creek near Iron Belt to create several lakes is made by the U.S. Department of the Interior.
- June 12-13: The milling and mining machinery of the Montreal Mine are auctioned off for $3,750,000
- July: Hurley celebrates White Way Days. Although the event draws thousands of people, it is reported it will be held in Ironwood next year because some residents object that they could not find adequate parking while in town due to the festival.
- August: Mercer Fibre Glass Product Company, a division of the Mercer Boat Company, develops a new high moisture grain storage bin made entirely of fiberglass.
- September 1: Universal Telephone, the new owner of the Mercer Suburban Telephone Company, activates dial telephones for the town.
- October: The threatened shutdown of the Twin City Iron Works is averted when it is purchased by the Iron County Area Development Corporation. The factory is leased by Malcom Foundry and Machine Company.
- October 19: The last ore from the Montreal Mine stockpile is shipped today.

1964
- January 8: Operations at the Cary Mine permanently cease, ending Iron county's iron mining era.
- April: The National Finnish American Festival, Inc. is organized in Hurley. A cultural center opens on July 5th in the Number 5 Dry Building in Montreal.
- May: A fire destroys the old Bowery and two other buildings on the corners of 2nd and Silver Street, sweeping away more of "old Hurley."
- June 5: The Saxon and Gurney schools join the Hurley School District.
- September: Camp Olympia in Upson is developed by Tom Rosandich, as a year-round sports facility.
- November: Wisconsin tax agents and the FBI crack down on vice operations in Hurley alleging that 25 exotic dancers were imported into Hurley for the deer season for soliciting drinks and prostitution.
- The Montreal Mining Office Building, built in 1913, is purchased by the Iron Gate Inn to serve as a lodging facility for skiers. It will be sold again, becoming the Montreal Academy, then the Montreal Inn.

1965
- April: Hurley will receive 3,300 gallons of paint, brushes, and rollers free from the Wisconsin Paint, Varnish, and Lacquer Company for a business and residential paint-up/fix-up beautification project. Choices are limited to three colors: white, cream, and gray.
- April: The Erspamer Super Market safe is blown, and $3,000-$4,000 is taken.
- May: The Odanah Mining Company turns over the Cary Mine building to the Iron County Area Resource Development Corporation for $1.00 for development purposes.
- June: A project is started to enlarge Saxon Harbor, install new breakwaters, and establish it as a safe refuge harbor.
- July: Amidst some secrecy, Erspamer Super Market buys an entire block in the heart of Silver Street's saloon district. Five taverns on the east end of the 200 block are demolished to make way for the new Erspamer Super Market. Gone are the "Finn" block of taverns, the New Central, Congress Bar, and several of the more colorful watering holes of the lower block. Local newspapers tout the move as "starting a new era for the lower block... for what goes on there affects the welfare of our town."
- October: Henry Kimball, owner of the Club 13 in Hurley, is shot to death on Hurley's lower block.
- November: 20 Hurley residents receive subpoenas to determine if a grand jury investigation is needed in the violation of federal laws affecting interstate transportation for the purpose of racketeering. Three arrests are made on charges of using interstate mail and telegraph facilities in the operation of a house of prostitution.

1966
- Aircraft Instruments Corporation becomes Hurley's newest industry in old Hurley City Hall building.
- Richard Plastics Company, Aurora, Illinois, joins Hurley Plastics Company and moves all of its operations to the old Cary Mine Building.
- The steel pilings and breakwater of reject chunks from the Mellen quarry are installed as the breakwater at Saxon Harbor.
- The new 6,600-yard Eagle Bluff Golf Course is taking shape. Ed Erspamer, president, claims that hole #13 will be the World's Largest Tee.
- September 24: Chief Alex Bobidosh of the Lac du Flambeau Chippewa formally reopens the Old Flambeau Trail. The trail has been retraced and marked again by the

Iron County Historical Society and is expected to be a tourism attraction and recreational trail.

1967
- Business leaders agree that it is better to have five smaller industries rather than one large one such as the mines.
- The long strike at White Pine Mine continues.
- The Mercer Sno-A-Go-Goers snowmobile club is organized.
- February: Lack of snow is blamed for the loss of millions of dollars in Range ski business.
- April: A mountain lion is reported roaming south of Hurley.
- October: Giovanoni's opens a new hardware store.
- The Mercer K-12 district is approved, but Presque Isle with its $6 million valuation is permitted to attach itself instead to the Lakeland School District.
- Look-Up Workshop, Hurley's sheltered workshop, moves into the old Erspamer Store.

1968
- A hemlock tree, determined to have been 250 years old when it was buried by the glacier 10,000 years ago, is unearthed during the construction of the Lakehead pipeline in Saxon.
- January: Fire destroys the rope tow shack at Eagle Bluff Ski Area.
- March 5: Iron County celebrates its 75th anniversary. There is talk about a possible merger with Ashland County from which Iron separated 75 years ago. The County's 75th anniversary history book is released.
- Iron county economic development groups are working hard to encourage taconite mining here.
- The Weinbrenner Shoe Factory in Kimball closes.
- Governor Warren Knowles opens Biathlon Games at Camp Olympia Sports Village.
- July 27: On its 50th anniversary, fire destroys the Hamilton Club in Montreal.
- December 13: The Mercer Wildlife and Wetlands Club, Iron County and Wisconsin create a new wetlands area called the Little Turtle Flowage.

1969
- January: Hurley Chamber of Commerce declares that the area economy is based on "white gold, not iron ore."
- February: Hurley records a total of 205 inches of snow to date.
- Twin City Foundry closes.
- Northern Chief Mining Company, which owns about 1/3 of the property in Hurley and almost 50 homes in Carey and Germania, will put its property up for sale.
- Tri-State Homes, Inc. will develop a 20,000 sq. ft. pre-fabricated home manufacturing plant in Mercer.
- News that Holiday Inn plans to build a 100-120 unit hotel in the Kimball-Hurley area around a newly developed artificial lake is called the most exciting development since the ore discoveries of 1884.
- Northern Highland State Bank chartered to form a bank in Mercer.
- August 16: The first Paavo Nurmi Marathon is held. Jay Dirksen of South Dakota led a pack of 75 runners with a time of 2:32:40.
- November: Johnson Silo and Lumber Company opens a new mill at the former Keith Jesse mill property in Mercer, employing 15 men.

1970
- County Population: 6,533.
- January: Eagle Bluff Ski Area to open and become Iron county's second downhill facility.
- March: Cedar Valley Mills, located in the old Cary Mine engine house, is now manufacturing cedar shakes.
- April: Tri-State Homes in Mercer constructs its first model home.
- August: The Iron County Board of Supervisors passes an ordinance governing rock and roll festivals.
- October: Bomb threat at the Hurley High School; students are sent home early.
- Tom LaBlonde and John Rudberg are developing an area in Kimball to be called Lake Michele.

1971
- Dress code is changed at the Hurley High School: A new ruling allows girls to wear slacks to school. Pantsuits or dress slacks may be worn. Jeans are not allowed.
- Passenger train service to Hurley ends.
- The winter of 1970-71 yields 274" of snow!
- March: Hurley's Club Carnival is destroyed by fire.
- May: Fire destroys two more Silver Street taverns: the Cactus Bar and the Outhouse.
- July: Fire wipes out Mercer Lumber Company.
- August: Hurley participates in a trial program by Wisconsin Telephone Company to recycle old phone books.
- September: A "spaceship" lands on the shores of Lake Michele. It is a Futuro II vacation house owned by developer Tom LaBlonde.
- October: Chet & Eva Haines donate $31,000 for the purchase of a new fire truck for Mercer.

1972
- Federal agents raid two nightclubs on Hurley's lower block on suspicion of interstate commerce for purposes relating to prostitution. Both clubs are destroyed by fire in 1973.
- March 1: The Hurley Holiday Inn opens!
- August 15: Iron county is declared a disaster area due to flood damage caused by 6" of rain falling in less than 24 hours.
- October 18: Hurley School District teachers go on strike and set up picket lines; students are sent home. The strike lasts only one day.

1973
- February: The Band Box bar destroyed by fire.
- May: Fires continue to consume lower Silver Street as the Club 13 and French Casino building burns down.
- June: The County Board discusses a plan to build new courthouse/jail over a 10-year period.
- The Superior American Homes plant in Kimball is manufacturing mobile homes.
- October: "Madman Joe" Koehmstedt opens the Country Store at the site of the old Van Buskirk Co-op in Oma.

1974
- February: Bids for the new county courthouse amount to $670,000. The general contractor is Nasi Construction Company
- May: Gurney constructs a new community building.
- June: A Hurley landmark, the Chris Strong beer warehouse, dating back to 1900, is razed.
- July: The Hurley dump is closed after 50 years of use.
- The Hurley Girls' Little League has its first season.
- A county snowmobile plan will provide over 350 miles of trails.

1975
- April 18: The #6 shaft at the Montreal Mine caves in, creating a hole 20 by 40 feet deep. A fence has been

erected to secure the area, but citizens express concern over the possibility of more subsidence.
- June 21: The new Iron County Courthouse is dedicated. Judge Francis Fassino marries the first couple in the new Courthouse, Gene Charles Lee and Christine Elizabeth Leitgeb. The first marriage license issued in the new Courthouse is for Kathie Tenlen and Dennis Munn, who receive the license for free, compliments of county Clerk George Reed.
- Labor Day Headline reads: "Five Dead, 8 Injured in Gruesome Accident" on Hwy. 51 near Layman's Creek, as a car hits a caravan of the Drifters Motorcycle Club.

1976
- The movement to create the Great State of Superior from the Upper Peninsula and parts of Northern Wisconsin gains momentum.
- May: Buildings are razed in Hurley to make room for the new post office, including the former Marble Hall which dates back to 1887.
- Summer: Bats invade downtown Hurley.
- July: Wisconsin orders Northern Chief Mining Company to fence off or fill in any mine openings or cave-ins. There have been nine cave-ins along a 1½ mile stretch on Hwy. 77 between Carey and Gile since 1970.
- July: The Iron County Clinic opens.
- July 4: United States Bicentennial celebration.
- September: A 24-year mystery concerning the disappearance of William Burton is officially closed when his former secretary affirms that she signed his will, allowing Burton to be legally declared dead by a Madison County, Illinois, Circuit Court Judge. Burton and his wife were last seen in a New York City hotel on December 7, 1952. Several explanations have been given for their disappearance including avoiding tax evasion charges, although it is said their former tax delinquencies were paid, and concern over the bombing of their home by underworld hoodlums.

1977
- September: Approval is given for the construction of a 70-bed skilled care facility, to be known as the Villa Maria Health Care Center.
- October: Copps Food Center opens in Hurley.

1978
- January 1: New Year's Day twins, Jereme and Jonathon, are born to Dave and Billi Tauer of Oma.
- March 15: The Hurley City Council debates whether or not to limit the number of Class B liquor licenses to 10 above the city's current 37 licenses. Some council members feel that there are already too many taverns in Hurley. Others, concerned about tourism loss, feel that if licenses are left unrestricted Hurley may "boom" again. When asked about the controversy, one skier said "There are enough bars, but not enough good ones or enough restaurants."
- May 20: A baseball field, part of Riccelli Park, is dedicated as the Felix Patritto Memorial Park.
- August: The Iron county Court becomes a "circuit court" as part of the reorganization of the Wisconsin Court System.
- Built in 1917, the late Matt Annala's round rock barn in Oma is nominated by the State Historical Society to the National Register of Historic Places.
- December Headline: "Unusual Accident: Plane hits car on Highway 51 near River Lake Inn, Mercer. No injuries."

1979
- April 20: Fire destroys the Show Bar.

- July 15: Herb Kinney retires after over 35 years of employment with the county in the UW-Extension and Forestry departments.
- October: North Star Beverage buys the Cary Mine building for its soft drink distribution business.

1980
- County Population: 6,730.
- January: An open house marks the opening of the new Villa Maria Health Care Center in Hurley, a 75-bed skilled nursing facility.
- June: Groundbreaking ceremonies are held for new apartment buildings in Mercer.
- October: Construction starts on the new Hurley Army Reserve Center.

1981
- February: The Iron County Senior Center opens in Hurley.
- May 21: The loon statue arrives in Mercer--"The Loon Capital."
- October: Gotta's Barn, a Gile landmark, burns down.
- November: Country Villa apartments open in Saxon.

1982
- Last train passes through Mercer.
- March: The Hurley School Board decides to close the Saxon School after the 1981-82 school year.
- October: After decades of silence, the bells are ringing again at the old Courthouse in Hurley as part of a restoration project of the Historical Society.

1983
- April Headline: "Iron County is "Land Rich - Cash Poor."
- July: A Chicago girl is bitten by a giant musky in Island Lake.
- November: Voluntary fingerprinting begins in the Hurley School District.

1984
- The City of Hurley celebrates its Centennial.
- February: A "grand opening" race is held to mark the dedication of the Montreal Area Jaycees' cross-country ski trail.
- Almost 100 years old, Hurley's Soo Line Depot is destroyed by fire.
- May: Iron County will have a full-time District Attorney, starting in 1985.

1985
- Summer: Construction begins on the new building for Iron county VFW Post 1580. Also under construction is the new Look-Up Workshop on Cary Road in Hurley.
- June: High winds and hail cause damage in Hurley.
September 19: Billy's Bar in Mercer is gutted by fire.

1986
- January 22: Citizens and businesses join forces and create the Hurley Downtown Development Corporation. Hurley's revitalization will include parking facilities, storefront designs, and streetscapes.
- The Year of Construction in Hurley: Iron Exchange Bank, Giovanoni Hardware, Memorial Building, and Quik Mart. Over $4 million dollars in private investments are made on Silver Street.
- March: The County Board approves the establishment of an all-terrain vehicle (ATV) trail system in Iron county. The first ATV rally is held July 11-13.
- August: Look-Up Workshop dedicates its new building and will now be known as Highline Corporation.

1987
- February: The City of Hurley is now an official national weather reporting station. Reporting instruments are set up at the Holiday Inn.
- April: The Hurley Army Reserve gets a distinguished award as it is picked as the best of 44 units in the 416th Engineering Command.
- An Oma man, Carroll Dean (C.D.) Murphy, accompanies a trade mission to China.

1988
- October: Groundbreaking for the new Art Unlimited sewing plant located in Hurley's Industrial Park.
- November: The Mercer High School Girls' Volleyball Team wins the Class C State Tournament!

1989
- January Headline: "Hurley City Council OK's Nudity in Taverns." As one resident says, "Hurley without a strip joint is like Rome without a Pope." On April 11, the council voted to ban nude activities.
- September 6: Iron county is approved as one of eight state development zones which will share $14 million in state tax credits.
- November: The old Erspamer Super Market building, on 5th Avenue and Hwy. 77, is razed to make room for the Iron County Clinic's new professional building.

1990
- County Population: 6,153.
- January 20: Grassroots efforts by economic development groups to bring State Travel Information Center to Iron county are rewarded when Governor Tommy Thompson announces that a facility will be constructed in Hurley near the U.S. 2 and Highway 51 interchange.
- A drug tip hotline is installed in the Sheriff's Department. August: The newly-renovated St. Mary's Catholic Church in Hurley is re-dedicated.
- October: The county Board approves a county sales tax of 0.5% to take effect April 1, 1991.
- Iron County gets "first rights" to Wisconsin Central's abandoned railroad line for a recreational trail.

1991
- The Wisconsin Department of Natural Resources sells the Upson Ranger Station to Iron County. The transfer of the facility will ensure that it will continue to be used to support forestry activities.
- State highway signs proclaim Iron county as a Bear Habitat Area. "Bear Crossing" signs are placed along U.S. Highway 2, Highway 51, and Highway 77.
- June: St. Mary's School closes.
- Groundbreaking is held for the new Hurley City Hall on 5th Avenue.
- June: The County Board becomes a 15-member body, a cut of four supervisors.
- August 11: Dedication ceremony is held for the new Hurley K-12 School, located on Range View Drive in Kimball.
- Scandinavian Log Homes is in full operation in the Town of Kimball.
- An addition to the Mercer School is under construction.
- October: A 2,000-gallon fuel oil spill cancels classes at the Mercer School for two days.

1992
- May: Iron County Clinic's new professional building opens for business in Hurley.
- The first graduating class of the new Hurley K-12 School is one of the smallest in years, only 35 graduates.
- June: A groundbreaking ceremony is held for the new State Information Center in Hurley, which will open in December.
- June: Trains are running again from Mellen to Hurley on the old Wisconsin Central tracks.
- July: Torrential rains and saturated soil cause flooding of the Montreal River. Volunteers sandbag homes in the "flats" area, and bridges are closed until water levels subside. The scene is reminiscent of a similar flood on the 4th of July weekend in 1949.
- Residential recycling begins in Iron county with the installation of recycling boxes in all municipalities.
- November: "Mercer Girls' Volleyball Team Repeats 1988 Feat: Capturing the State Title!"

1993
- January: Cory Winn of Montreal submits the winning Centennial logo.
- February 2: Cathy Techtmann, Iron County Resource Agent, delivers the first draft of the Iron County Centennial Book to the publisher, Michael Goc, of New Past Press, Inc. Special thanks to Extension Secretary Linda Ryskewecz for burning the midnight oil to get the manuscript proofread.
- March 3: Iron County is 100 years old. Nelle Kopacz of the Iron County Historical Society blows out the candles on the County's birthday cake.
- June 1- August 8: The official Iron County Centennial celebration will be observed with special events throughout the county.
- June 7-9: Iron County hosts State Highway Conference.
- July 23-25: The official **Iron County Centennial Homecoming** will be held. Parades, picnics, fireworks and more is planned. Everyone is welcome to help celebrate Iron County's 100th Birthday!

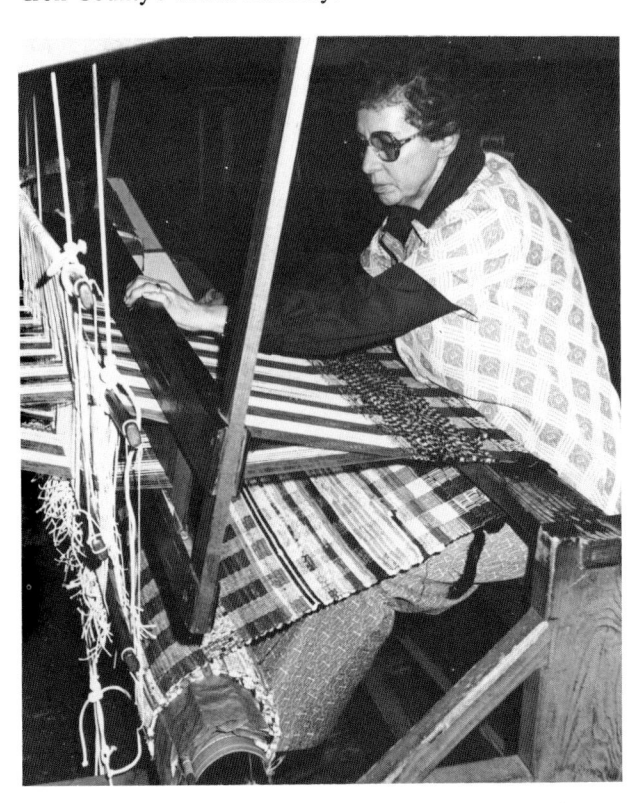

Hurley, c. 1990. Nelle Kopacz at the loom of the Iron County Historical Society. Without the work of volunteers like Kopacz, the history of Iron county would not have been preserved for publication in this book.

Index
Individuals

Ahlgrim, Bill, 74
Ahlgrim, Ernie, 74
Aimone, Elizabeth, 124
Allen, Bill, 62
Allen, Elizabeth, 62
Allen, Frank, 62
Anderson, Albert, 87
Anderson, J.B., 118
Annala, Matt, 68, 156
Appleyard, A.E., 147
Ashe, Dr. Henry, 152
Backlund, Walter, 101
Baird, Dr., 152
Baird, Mrs. 152
Banks, Rev. D.S., 83
Barncard, Sgt. Earl, 152
Baron, James, 132
Barto, Anna, 128
Barto, Louis, 128
Beariblund, A., 151
Beierle, Ella K., 153
Bennett, D.C., 147
Benson, Eleda, 103
Bertagnoli, Lt. George, 151
Bertagnoli, Clement, 138
Bino, John Sr., 153
Bobidosh, Alex, 154
Boisoneau, Eugene, 103
Borgiasz, Edward Borgi, 142
Brackett, Earl, 138
Brandt, Debbie, 96
Bresnahan, Pam, 101
Bresnahan, Robert, 101
Bridgeman, William H., 147
Brockman, Bertha, 56
Brown, Mrs. Ed, 69
Brunele, Sgt. Harry, 153
Brunner, Frank, 40
Bueschel, Ted, 73
Bugni, Anton, 9
Burton, John, 43, 146, 147
Burton, William, 156
Butterbrodt, Jim, 100
Carjala, Teda, 110
Carjola, Bill, 110
Carna, C.H., 146
Carow, W.S., 153
Chartier, Ben, 61
Chenoweth, Mrs. Hayes, 77
Chiapusio, John, 149
Chiapusio, Tony, 25
Christensen, Carl, 103
Cisewski, Walter, 150
Clark, C.R., 146
Comiskey, Charles, 108, 148
Conners, Matt, 58
Consie, A., 60
Constantini, Pvt. Fino, 151
Corrigan, Joe, 19
Cossette, Edward L., 148
Coxey, Shirley, 121
Cram, Thomas, 144
Crego, Herman, 31
Davis, George, 57
Davis, Ed, 44
Davis, Tom, 136
Day, Terry, 103
Dean, Carroll (C.D.), 157
Defer, J.J., 51, 140
DeRosso, H.A., 153
Detrick, Bill, 58
Dicky, Hanford, 87
Dietz, E.H., 33, 38, 39, 41, 150
Dillinger, John, 103
Eaver, J.C., 50

Egan, Tim, 58
Eilo, Oscar, 129
Elliot, Mrs., 72
Emerson Brothers, 18
Emerson, D.W., 142, 147
Emerson, John, 142
Emunson, F.A., 148
Erspamer, Dick, 61
Erspamer, Fred, 61
Erspamer, Herman, 61
Erspamer, Robert, 24
Erspamer, Ted, 124
Evenson, "Big" Ed, 40, 57, 149
Falconio, Rev. De Medio, 83
Fassino, Francis, 156
Flannagan, John, C. 113
Flateau, Vincent, 87
Folsom, Fannie, 147
Gamache, Thomas, 124
Gamache, Thomas, 152
Gehr, Lee, 65
Gene, Val, 121
Gilbert, Father, 77, 146
Goodell, Mr., 145
Gowdey, Mr., 145
Grey, Depotmaster, 140, 146
Grew, Lucia, 87
Gudlewski, Andrew, 149
Hagen, E.S. 88
Hakala, Ed, 33, 121
Hand, F.A., 145
Hanley, William, 146
Hanneman, Walt, 20
Hannula, Heino, 38
Hannula, Thomas, 136
Hantula, Lucy Luoma, 34
Hardenburgh, L.M., 120
Hardy, Emil, 110
Harper, Charlie, 44, 56, 71
Harper, Ida, 56
Harries, Rev. C.L., 83
Harries, Mrs. C.L., 152
Hayers, Mrs., 146
Hayes, E.A., 22, 144
Hayes, J.O., 22, 144
Hayward, Mert, 19
Hiener, Walt, 87
Hoffman, William, 72
Hogan, R.D., 122
Holger, Warren, 154
Hosley, Gus, 15
Hurley, Michael Angelo "Glen," 145
Husen, Frank, 77
Innes, Bob, 33
Innes, Tom, 122
Jackson, August, 63
Jaunti, "Toots," 40
Jensen, W.C., 123
Jesse, Keith, 74, 153
Jewell, Bessie, 77
Johnson, William, 79
Kapenen, Leonard, 28
Kauppi, Otto, 58
Kennedy, John F., 154
Ketcham, Rev. Edward, 154
Kimball, A.M., 126
Kimball, Henry, 154
Kinney, Herb, 156
Kivi, Matti, 147
Kluggin, Bernie, 40
Knight, John, 128
Knowles, Warren, 155
Koehmstedt, "Madman Joe," 155
Kolu, Gust, 121
Kopacz, Nelle, 157
Koshak, Al, 65
Krall, Mike, 121

LaBlonde, Tom, 155
Langford, Richard, 144
Lantta, Fred, Jr., 128
LaPorte, Grandpa, 49
LeClaire, Charles, 88
Lee, Blanche, 91
Lee, Gene Charles, 156
LeFevre, Joseph, 31
Leichtnam, Joe, 87
Leitgeb, Christine Elizabeth, 156
Lennon, Patrick, 146
Lewis, Gus, 62
Logan, Frank, 128
Long, Neil, 40
Luby, Leola, 77
Lucia, Erb., 87
Lucia, Grew, 87
Lugviel, Carl, 58
Lypi, Syma, 110
Maffesanti, Frank "Kluchie," 100
Malhoit, Francois Victor, 13
Marta, Frank, 147
Mason, Byron, 19
Mattei, Noel, 107
Mattson, Matt, 121
McConnell, T., 151
McCrossen, Dan, 145
McDonald, Tom, 63
McPhail, Dan, 63
McVichie, D., 128
Meade, Henry 59, 124
Merrill, George, 146
Meyers, Catherine, 146
Moffat, Charles, 79
Montalban, Ricardo, 154
Moon, V.A., 149
Moore, Nathaniel, 22
Morgan, Lotta, 103
Morris, John, 38, 151
Munn, Dennis, 156
Murhpy, J.E., 77, 153
Murray, Dave, 60
Neibuhr, Frederick, 58
Nelson, Alec, 69
Nelson, Arvid, 121
Nevala, Jack, 45
Newman, Paul, 154
Nicholson, Kathleen, 77, 146
Nicholson, Nellie, 146
Niemi, Axel, 14
Niemi, Bucky, 30
Niemi, Harold, 30, 98
Niemi, Martin, 98
Niemi, Nestor, 30
Niemi, Paul, 12
Niemi, Werner, 98
Nuono, Father Gilbert, 83
Nurmi, Paavo, 95
Nyman, Charles, 147
Olson, John, 36
Otte, Kenneth, 120
Owen, D.D., 144
Patritto, Felix, 156
Patterson, Dr. R.C., 154
Pelto, Pvt. Julianna, 152
Pelto, Cpl. Toivo, 152
Peterson, Buckley, 153
Peterson, Mrs., 153
Peterson, Sally Rae, 153
Pierrelee, Jean, 118
Pierson, James, 151
Pollard, Michael, 154
Pollock, Florence Secor, 58
Potter, Lewis A., 103
Price, John M., 132
Pripps, Bernhard, 142, 147
Pripps, Lulu, 142
Prosek, Carl, 126

Raabe, John, 130
Rautio, Lt. David, 152
Rautio, Sam, 154
Reardon, John, 58
Reible, Amelia, 77
Rein, John, 136
Richardson, George, 130, 147
Robbins, R.E., 132
Roberts, George, 72
Roberts, Richard, 69
Roddis, William Henry, 16
Rowe, Robert, 140
Rudberg, John, 155
Ruggles, Alba, 59
Rundell, Andrew, 160
Ryan, Paddy, 57
Ryskewecz, Linda, 157
Schomberg, Richard , Jr., 150
Schoolcraft, Henry, 11
Schwartz, Carrie, 147
Schwartz, George, 44
Secor, David, 152
Secor, Matt, 152
Seifert, Alberta, 153
Shaffer, Dan, 31, 33, 149
Shea, Dan, 20
Shep, 103
Sigler, Emma, 149
Sigler, Andrew, 149
"Smokey Bear," 40
Sohl, Robert, 152
Sola, John, 34
Stahl, Mr. 140
Staples, E.H., 20
Stone, Bernie, 49
Stone, Horton, Jr., 49
Stone, H.J., 49
Stone, Levisa, 49
Strobel, George, 24
Summers, Miss, 77, 146
Sunie, Tovio, 149
Surprise, H., 145
Swanson, Mr., 145
Tandy, Jessica, 154
Tarrish, Henry 103
Tauer, Billi, 156
Tauer, Dave, 156
Tauer, Jereme, 156
Tauer, Jonathon, 156
Techtmann, Cathy 157
Tenlen, Kathie, 156
Thomas, Edith, 145
Thomas, Judge Griff, 103
Thompson, First Lt. Lloyd, 152
Thompson, Tommy, 157
Trier, Luella, 114
Vallone, George, 34
Van Buskirk Brothers, 116, 145
VanSchaick, A.G., 149
Verwyst, Father Chrysostom, 83
Wallach, Eli, 154
Walli, Matt, 69
Walter, William, 61
Weber, Anne, 79, 147
Weber, William, 126
White, Peter, 147
Whitefield, Mr., 145
Whitefield, W.H., 151
Whittlesey, Charles, 144
Wilson, Jeff, 36
Winn, Cory, 157
Woitkielewicz (Woit), Adam, 151
Wolfe, Jane, 69
Wolfe, Phil, 69
Zinsmaster, Charlie, 100

Index
Groups

Sackett Family, 10
Conservation Corps, 1986, 41
Oddino Family, 46
Kimball Family, 69
Maggie May School, 1910, 78
First Hurley High School Graduates, 1893, 78
VanBuskirk School Children, 1900, 78
Gurney School Children, 1952, 80
4-H Youth and Leaders, 1992, 81
Upson Baseball Team, 1913-14, 87
Garibaldi and Providente Societies, 1907, 90
Order of Owls, 1900, 91
Hurley High School Football Team, 1902, 92
Hurley High School Basketball Champs, 1949, 92
Hurley High School Girls Basketball Team, 1924, 93
Mercer High School Girls Basketball Team, 1916, 93
Mercer High School Boys Basketball Team, 1916, 93
"Battling Bruisers," 95
Cast, "Adventures of A Young Man," 108
"Famous People Who Visited, 109
Died In Service, 111
Carey Road Crew, 1920, 114
County Officials, Then and Now, 115
County Supervisors, 1992-94, 115
Springstead School Children, 1964, 143
Carey Town Board, 1919, 121
Into Finnish Athletic Club, 127
Friends from Pence, 1912, 138

Maps, Charts, Lists

Iron Mines, 1881, 23
County Forests, 39
Silver Street, 1900, 54
Downtown Mercer, 1900-09, 56
Newspapers, Hurley, 75
Lost Communities, 116

For Further Reading

100 Years on the Flambeau, Park Falls Centennial Committee. 1989.
Call It North Country, John Bartlow Martin. 1953.
Caulked Boots and Cant Hooks, George A. Corrigan. 1976
Early Hurley, Craig A. Lewis. 1984.
History of Gogebic County, Victor Lemmer. 1955.
History of Ironwood, Ironwood Centennial Paper. 1985
Hurley Centennial Paper. 1984
Hurley, Still No Angel, Lewis C. Reimann. 1954
I Married a Logger, Julie Anderson. 1951
Iron County History (WPA Project #6555). 1985
Iron County's 75th Anniversary Edition (Diamond Jubilee). 1968
Ironwood, Michigan and Surrounding Area: Like It Usta Was, Earle Sell. 1990
Looking Back--Moving Forward, Ashland Centennial Task Force. 1987
Our Heritage, Joseph Gill.
Vein of Iron, Walter Havighurst. 1958

Afterword

"I had been accustomed to seeing the sun above me, but now it was between me and the water--on the water and under the water, and now the sun sleeps in Lake Superior... and so we too come to the end of a perfect day, made so by those in the past planning for the future which for us is today and from now on. Let us make the most of it, but jealously guard what we have so we can pass it on to be enjoyed by those who will follow in our footsteps".

Diary of Andrew Rundell, 1846, as he stood on Lake Superior's shore.

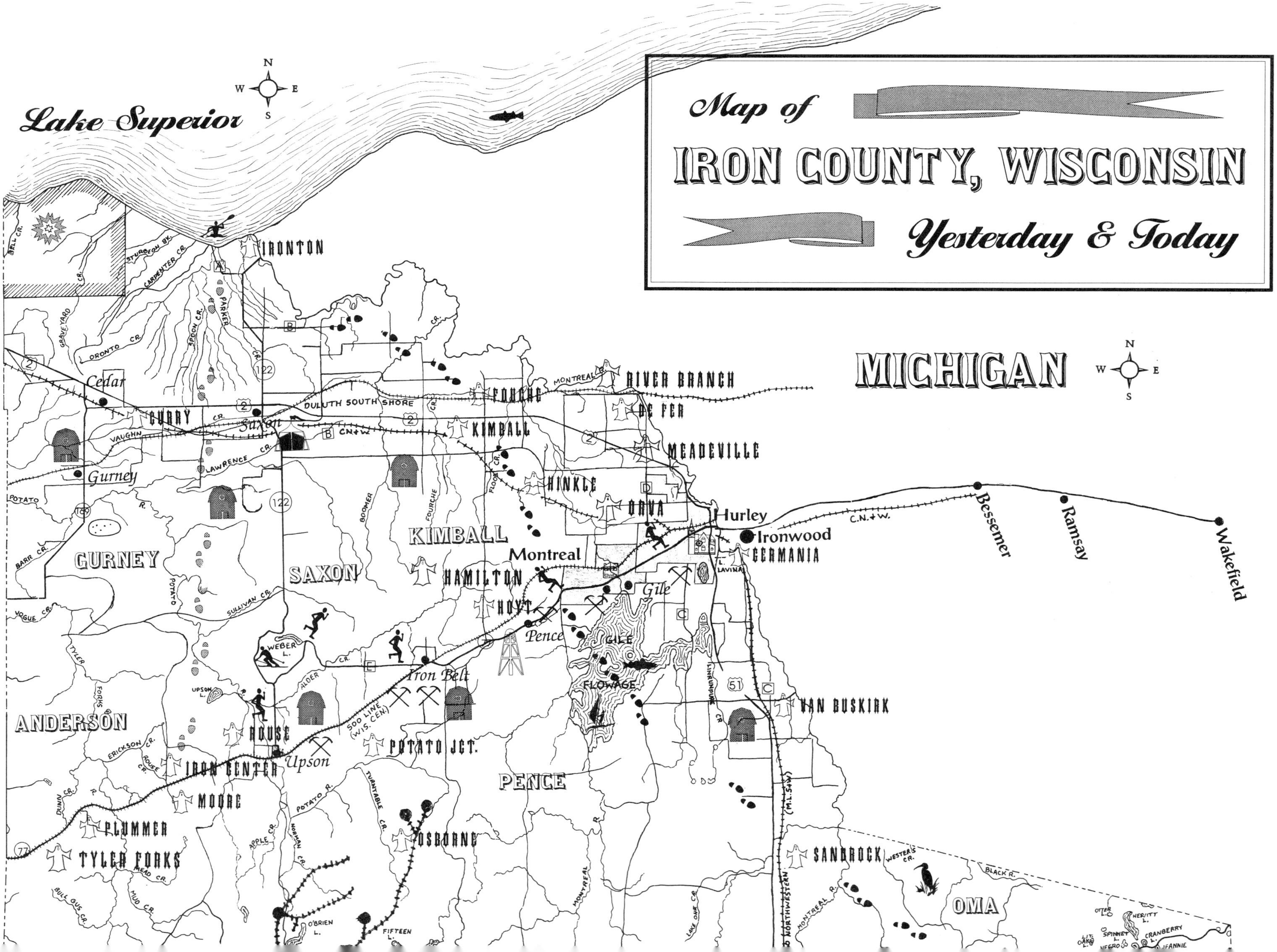
Map of
IRON COUNTY, WISCONSIN
Yesterday & Today
Lake Superior
MICHIGAN
IRONTON
RIVER BRANCH
FOURCHE
DE FER
KIMBALL
MEADEVILLE
HINKLE
ORVA
Hurley
Ironwood
GERMANIA
Bessemer
Ramsay
Wakefield
C.N.+W.
Montreal
HAMILTON
HOYT
Pence
Gile
GILE
FLOWAGE
Iron Belt
SAXON
Saxon
CURRY
Cedar
Gurney
GURNEY
ANDERSON
ROUSE
Upson
IRON CENTER
POTATO JCT.
PENCE
VAN BUSKIRK
MOORE
PLUMMER
TYLER FORKS
OSBORNE
SANDROCK
OMA
DULUTH SOUTH SHORE
SOO LINE (WIS. CEN.)
NORTHWESTERN (M.L.S.W)
WEBER L.
UPSON L.
O'BRIEN L.
FIFTEEN L.
LAVINA L.
MONTREAL R.
BOOMER
FOURCHE
FLOOR CR.
SULLIVAN CR.
LAWRENCE CR.
VAUGHN
PARKER
SPOON CR.
ORONTO CR.
GRAVEYARD
CARPENTER CR.
STURGEON BK.
BELL CR.
BARR CR.
VOGUE CR.
POTATO R.
TYLER FORKS
ERICKSON CR.
ROUSE CR.
DUNN CR.
MEAD CR.
MUD CR.
BILL GUS CR.
APPLE CR.
NORMAN CR.
TURNTABLE CR.
ALDER CR.
LINRUNPUKE CR.
LAKE ONE CR.
WESTER'S CR.
BLACK R.
OTTER L.
HERITT L.
SPINNET L.
CRANBERRY L.
FANNIE
2
122
169
77
51
A
B
C
D
E